TWAYNE'S WORLD LEADERS SERIES

EDITORS OF THIS VOLUME

Arthur W. Brown

Baruch College, The City University
of New York

and

Thomas S. Knight

Adelphi University

Descartes

TWLS 63

"Descartes as a Young Man," anonymous,
Musée des Augustins, Toulouse.

DESCARTES

By LEON PEARL

Hofstra University

TWAYNE PUBLISHERS
A DIVISION OF G. K. HALL & CO., BOSTON

Library of Congress Cataloging in Publication Data

Pearl, Leon
    Descartes.

    (Twayne's world leaders series ; TWLS 63)
    Bibliography: pp. 223–24
    Includes index.
    1. Descartes, René, 1596–1650.
B1875.P33   194   76–54502
ISBN 0-8057-7714-8

To My Children
Janet
Barry
Kenneth
Carl

Contents

About the Author

Leon Pearl was born in 1922 in Poland, migrated to the U.S. at age six and served in the armed forces in the second World War. He attended Brooklyn College, U.C.L.A. and received his Ph.D. from N.Y.U. in 1957. He has held teaching positions in Brooklyn College, C.C.N.Y. and is presently professor of philosophy at Hofstra University.

Leon Pearl wrote *Four Philosophical Problems* (Harper and Row, 1963). His articles have appeared in *Mind*, *Monist* and *Philosophy and Phenomenological Research*.

Preface

This book is an introduction to the philosopher, mathematician and scientist, René Descartes. While written primarily for the reader who is not trained in philosophy, it is sufficiently scholarly to be of value to students of Descartes. With the exception of the first two and last two chapters, this work is a commentary on the *Meditations*, a work which ranks with Plato's *Republic* and Immanuel Kant's *Critique of Pure Reason* as one of the truly great classics of philosophy. The reader of the *Meditations* is taken by Descartes on an intellectual journey of discovery. Two reasons make this journey exciting. First, Descartes takes nothing for granted; at one point, for instance, he considers the possibility that he might never have been awake. Secondly, Descartes employs persuasive arguments for conclusions which, to most people, would appear to be conspicuously false. He argues, for instance, for the position that sensations of pain and hunger are not located in any of the parts of organic bodies.

In writing this book I owe much to many people but shall simply mention those to whom I owe the most. My interest in Descartes is due to the influence of my friend and colleague, Joseph LaLumia. In reading the works of Harry Frankfurt and Anthony Kenny, I have learned much about Descartes, though I disagree with some of their interpretations. I also wish to acknowledge the invaluable assistance of the editors of this volume, Dean Arthur W. Brown and Professor Thomas S. Knight. I owe a debt to Mrs. Mary Frances Klerk, the secretary of the Hofstra Philosophy Department, for her patience and understanding in working with me on the manuscript.

LEON PEARL

Hofstra University

Chronology

CHAPTER 1

Descartes' Life

I *Birth*

RENÉ Descartes was born March 31, 1596, in the French province of Touraine, into a family which belonged to the *Noblesse de la Robe*, a class situated between the nobility and the bourgeoisie. His grandfather Pierre was a medical practitioner and his father Joachim was a counselor to the Parliament of Brittany. René was the last of four children, and since his mother died in childbirth a year after his birth, he was brought up by his grandmother and a nurse. Fortunately for Descartes, his family was well-to-do, and he was able to live without financial concerns.

When Descartes was ten years old, he was enrolled at La Flèche, a Jesuit school founded two years earlier by the French king Henri IV, where he was to remain until his nineteenth year. In the first six years, he studied the humanities, and developed a love of poetry which stayed with him in the years immediately following his schooling. In later life, however, he was to consider book reading of any sort a hindrance in his quest for knowledge. In the last three years at La Flèche, his studies consisted of philosophy and mathematics. The reader, regarding this matter, should keep in mind two facts. First, the term "philosophy" was not confined, as it is today, to logic, ethics, and metaphysics but also covered the natural sciences and psychology as well; and second, the physics, psychology, and metaphysics taught at La Flèche were primarily that of Aristotle and his medieval commentators. The new current of mathematical physics, ushered in by Galileo and Kepler, had as yet no impact on the Jesuit schools. In mathematics, however, Descartes' studies were more up-to-date, for he learned

13

not only the geometry of the ancients but the algebra of the moderns as well.

Descartes was an exceptionally good student with a high opinion of his Jesuit teachers, an opinion which he was to retain the rest of his life, and without the slightest doubt that his education was the best that was available at that time in any European school. Nevertheless, in one respect, La Flèche was a disappointment to Descartes; for with the exception of mathematics, he felt that he had learned nothing which he could, with absolute certainty, claim to be true. The contrast between the mathematics and the philosophy which he studied at La Flèche was destined to play a major role in the later development of his thinking. In the *Discourse* Descartes, as a mature thinker, looks back and describes how this contrast impressed him as a student:

Most of all was I delighted with mathematics, because of the certainty of its demonstrations and the evidence of its reasoning; but I did not yet understand its use, and, believing that it was of service only in the mechanical arts, I was astonished that, seeing how firm and solid was its basis, no loftier edifice has been reared thereupon.[1]

The certain knowledge provided by mathematics was then contrasted with philosophy:

I shall not say anything about philosophy, but that, seeing that it had been cultivated for many centuries by the best minds that have ever lived, and that nevertheless no single thing is to be found in it which is not a subject of dispute, and in consequence which is not dubious . . .[2]

But there is likely to have been another reason for the youthful Descartes to have been disappointed with the sciences (philosophy) of his day. They had no practical utility. They were purely speculative and did not provide any benefits to mankind. What Descartes sought was a philosophy which would provide human beings with power over nature and which would lead to the elimination of disease and the elongation of life. He wrote:

... it is possible to attain knowledge which is very useful in life, and that instead of that speculative philosophy which is taught in the schools, we may find a practical philosophy by means of which, knowing the force and the action of fire, water, air, the stars, heavens, and all other bodies that environ us, as distinctly as we know the different crafts of our artisans, we can in the same way employ them in all those uses to which they are adopted and thus render ourselves the masters and possessors of nature.[3]

Descartes' disappointment with his studies at La Flèche was twofold. On the one hand, he notes there is mathematics, which undoubtedly contains knowledge but seems to be of little use except in servicing the mechanical arts; on the other hand, there is philosophy which is supposed to provide human beings with knowledge but which, unfortunately, provides them with neither. Already in his disappointment there is contained the seed for the subsequent development of one of the major themes in his philosophy. The position he was to adopt was that a true and practical science of nature involves the application of mathematical concepts to concrete phenomenon. The book of nature is, so to speak, written in the language of mathematics.

Because of his disappointment at La Flèche, Descartes decided to abandon his study of the sciences and become "a man of the world." He felt that by observing the decisions men make in practical affairs, where errors of judgment, unlike those committed by philosophers, can lead to calamities, he might learn some significant truth that would be useful in the conduct of his life. He writes:

I employed the rest of my youth in travel, in seeing courts and armies, in intercourse with men of diverse temperaments and conditions, in collecting varied experiences. . . . For it seemed to me that I might meet with much more truth in the reasonings that each man makes on the matters that specially concern him, and the issue of which would very soon punish' him if he made a wrong judgment, than in the case of those made by a man of letters in his study touching speculations which lead to no result . . .[4]

Unfortunately, what Descartes called "the book of the world" proved no less frustrating than the philosophical texts he studied at La Flèche; for, as he was to record later in life, "I remarked in them [meaning the opinions of the practical men of the world] almost as much diversity as I had formerly seen in the opinions of philosophers."[5] The two passages above refer to the period of Descartes' life from 1616 to 1619. We know very little about Descartes' life during this period. We have evidence that he left La Flèche in November, 1614, and that he received his degree in law in Poitiers in November, 1616. Sometime in 1618 he volunteered, without pay, in the army of Prince Maurice of Nassau, who was fighting the Spanish armies in Holland. In April, 1619, he resigned from the army, sailed from Amsterdam to Copenhagen and then to the port city of Danzig, from which he started his travels through Poland, Bohemia, and Austria, reaching the German city of Frankfurt in time to witness the coronation of Emperor Frederick. Subsequently, he joined as a volunteer in the army of the Catholic Duke Maximilian of Bavaria. On November 10, 1619, Descartes had three consecutive dreams which he attributed to divine inspiration and which were to affect the subsequent course of his whole life. In the *Discourse* he described the occurrence in a rather matter-of-fact way:

When, however, I had occupied some years in thus studying the book of the world, and in striving to widen the range of my experience, I one day resolved to take myself too as an object of study and to employ all the powers of my mind in choosing the paths I should follow; and in this way I succeeded, as it seems to me, far better than I could have done had I never quitted my country or put aside my books.[6]

II   *The Awakening*

The new turn in Descartes' life, which was to have far-reaching consequences not only for his life but for the subsequent history of human thought, began when he met Isaac Beeckman, rector at Dortmund, whose interests were in mathematics and physics. It will be recalled that, upon leaving La Flèche, Descartes believed that the usefulness of mathematics was confined to the mechanical arts; and in fact as a military officer, before meeting Beeckman, Descartes' sole use of mathe-

matics was in solving problems in ballistics and military archi-
tecture. It was Beeckman who introduced Descartes to the new
mathematical physics which was challenging the Scholastic and
Aristotelean natural science. This in turn led to a widening
and deepening of Descartes' work in mathematics and was
correctly recognized by him as a turning point in his intellectual
development; writing in appreciation to Beeckman a year later,
he says: "Whenever I tarry, I promise to start at once the
composition of my mechanics or geometry, and to laud you
as my inspiration and spiritual mentor . . . you alone have shaken
my idleness from me."[7]

Shortly after meeting Beeckman, Descartes discovered coordinate geometry. The main idea involved in this new discipline
is that for each curve there is a corresponding algebraic equation that uniquely describes the points of the curve and, conversely, each equation involving the variables X and Y can
be pictured as a curve by considering X and Y to be coordinates
of points. Thus, by combining algebra and geometry, Descartes
found a method for solving a number of difficult mathematical
problems. It was characteristic of Descartes' philosophical bent
of mind to consider his work in coordinate geometry as illus-
trating some principle about mathematics in general which he
called "universal mathematics":

But as I considered the matter carefully, it gradually came to light
that all these matters only were referred to mathematics in which
order and measurement are investigated, and that it makes no difference whether it be in numbers, figures, stars, sounds or any other
object that the question of measurement arises.[8]

For the intellectually bold and fertile mind of Descartes, it
was but a short step from his conception of universal mathematics to that of a method which applies to all the sciences;
in other words, to philosophy in general. Descartes, contrary to
common opinion, was not interested in mathematics for its own
sake. His purpose for working in that discipline was not to
study the properties of "sterile numbers and imaginary figures"
but rather to train his mind in the mastery of a method which
could then be employed in making discoveries in those sciences

which he termed "philosophical." Mathematics is not the method, but the first product of the method. He writes:

Those long chains of reasoning, simple and easy as they are, of which geometricians make use in order to arrive at the most difficult demonstrations, had caused me to imagine that all those things which fall under the cognizance of man might very likely be mutually related in the same fashion . . .[9]

Descartes now had a clear view of his future task; he was to explicate and articulate the method employed in mathematical reasoning and then apply it to metaphysics and the natural sciences. But was he capable of performing the task? His state of mind immediately preceding November 10, 1619, fluctuated between enthusiasm for his new mission in life and feelings of depression due to self-doubt. Then on November 10, he had the three previously mentioned dreams.[10]

In the first dream a wind is whirling him about in the street as he tries to reach the church of the college to say his prayers. Upon noticing that he has passed a man with whom he was acquainted without having greeted him, he tries to return, but the wind will not allow him. He then sees another man standing in the college courtyard who tells him that an acquaintance of his is in the church and has a melon to give him. Descartes then awakens; feeling pain, he concludes that his dream was the work of an evil demon and prays to God for protection. After an interval of two hours, Descartes again falls asleep and in his new dream it seems to him that he hears a loud and piercing sound, which he takes to be a clap of thunder. He immediately awakens and, upon opening his eyes, he sees thousands of fiery sparks in the room. In the third and final dream, he finds on his table a dictionary and a collection of poems entitled *Corpus Poetarum*, and upon opening the latter volume, he notices the line, *Quod vitae sectabor iter?* ("What path shall I follow in life?"). A man he does not know presents him with verses which begin with the words *est et non* ("yes and no").

What is amazing is that, while he was dreaming, he not only realized that he was dreaming but proceeded to interpret the dream. The dictionary stood for all the various sciences as a collective body; the *Corpus Poetarum* marked in a distinct manner the union of philosophy and wisdom, and the *est et non* was the yes and no of Pythagoras which stood for truth and error in human knowledge.

When Descartes woke up, he concluded that all three dreams were due to the spirit of truth which God sent to him. The first two were a warning regarding his past life, which was, in his opinion, not blameless before the eyes of God. The last one was encouragement for what he took to be the mission of his life, namely, to set the sciences on the right path to knowledge. We are now in the position to understand what Descartes most likely meant when he wrote: "I one day resolved to take myself too as an object of study...."[11] The right method for the sciences was identified by Descartes with "the natural light of reason" or what to him amounted to the same thing, the use of human intelligence in the conduct of inquiry. Consequently, he made it his mission, as dictated by his third dream, to devote his life to study the function of his faculty of reason as it operates on a variety of subjects. This was Decartes' interpretation of Socrates' famous maxim, "Know Thyself."

In the years from 1619 to 1628 Descartes continued his travels, visiting France in 1622. He sold his estates in Poitou. His family tried to persuade him to marry and settle down; but he declined, claiming, according to tradition, that there is no beauty comparable to the beauty of truth. After leaving France, he traveled in Italy from 1623 to 1625. In Italy he fulfilled his vow, which he had made upon awakening from his dreams, of a pilgrimage to Loreto. He then returned to France and spent two years in Paris in the company of such men of science as the astronomer Jean Baptiste Morin and the mathematician Claude Mydorge. It was also at this time that Descartes developed a strong friendship with Marin Mersenne, who was later to become his chief communicant with the scholars of the time. In the fall of 1628 Descartes retired to Holland, where he was to remain, with the exception of three short visits to France in 1644, 1647 and 1648, until he left for Sweden in September, 1649. Descartes left Paris because he did not like it. The air of that city, he writes, "makes me dream instead of thinking philosophical thoughts. There I see so many men who are mistaken in their opinions and in their calculations that I am of the opinion that there is there a universal sickness."[12] True, he had made friends in Paris and enjoyed holding philosophical conversations with them, but, given his aversion to the city and his love of solitude, he decided to leave.

What was Descartes' intellectual development from 1619 to his retirement in Holland? We know that he was working out the details of his method which in 1628 he set down in writing under the title, *Regulae Ad Directionem Ingenii* (*Rules for the Direction of the Mind*), posthumously published in 1701. This work not only contains—in the form of twenty-one rules—a much more detailed presentation of Descartes' method than is to be found in his later and more famous work, *The Discourse on Method*, but also some of the metaphysical ideas that he was to develop further in his later writings. Also in this period Descartes was occupied in the study of natural science. There is reason to believe that some of the ideas, for instance, that the essential nature of body is to be extended in length, breadth, and depth, which were to appear in his work *On the World*, were developed at this time.

III   *The Mature Period*

The years 1628 to 1649 are the mature period of Descartes' thinking. During this time he started working in the area of physiology and visited daily the slaughterhouses of Amsterdam to study the anatomy of animals and to carry out dissections on their various parts. One of the problems which scholars of the works of Descartes face is that there appears to be a contradiction between the master's theory that all the sciences should adopt the *a priori* method of pure mathematics, where propositions are not tested for their truth or falsehood by experience, and his making detailed observations of animal bodies in order to study their physiological mechanisms.

Also at this time Descartes became concerned with a number of problems. His attempts at solving them were incorporated in the major works which he wrote at this period. Nature, according to Descartes, is not as it appears to our sense experience.

Things are not what they seem to be [handwritten annotation]

To our senses, bodies appear to have color, heat, and sound. Not so, claims Descartes; bodies have only geometrical properties and motion; and all the changes that they undergo, contrary to what seems to be the case to our sense experience, are purely quantitative. But then Descartes faced the problem—what are color, heat, sound, and smell, which we experience? What accounts for the fact that they appear to us as properties of bodies? In other words, what is the relation between the mechanistic, purely quantitative world of mathematical physics and the colored world of our daily experience? Another problem which Descartes had to confront was the relation of his philosophy of nature to the two basic beliefs of the Christian religion, namely, the existence of God and the survival of the soul after death. For the Scholastics, knowledge of God's existence was inferred from certain alleged facts which belonged to an Aristotelean conception of nature. But if this conception is rejected, as it was by Descartes, what then constitutes the basis for belief in God's existence? Descartes, as a devout Christian, could not ignore this issue. "I have always," he writes to the faculty of theology in Paris, "considered that the two questions respecting God and the Soul were the chief of those that ought to be demonstrated in philosophical rather than theological argument."[13] Still another problem which confronted Descartes was whether human knowledge was possible. The two skeptics, Michel de Montaigne and Pierre Charron, had argued that human beings could never be in a position where they could be certain that they had knowledge of any sort, including knowledge of mathematics. Since their writings, during this period of Descartes' life, exerted a great influence on the educated public, Descartes felt obliged, if he was going to set the sciences on the right path, to meet their challenge.

In broad outline these are some of the problems which Descartes incorporated in his major works. In 1633 Descartes finished writing his treatise *On the World*, which consisted of his theories in physiology, perception, physics, and cosmology, including the Copernican hypothesis of the earth's motion around the sun. He then heard from his friend Marin Mersenne in Paris that the Catholic Church had recently condemned Galileo for advancing the Copernican hypothesis. Being a cautious man, and a good son of the church, Descartes decided to withhold publishing the manuscript. Some of the ideas in *On the World* were incorporated in some of his later works. In 1637 a publishing house in Leyden printed Descartes' epoch-making work which had the long title *Discourses on the Method of Properly Guiding the Reason in the Search for Truth in the Sciences. Also the Dioptric, the Meteors, and the Geometry, Which are Essays in this Method.* From the title it is apparent that Descartes not only stated some of the main principles of his method but also intended to display their usefulness in solving problems in physics and geometry. The *Discourse* was the first scholarly work in Europe which was not written in Latin. As a French literary masterpiece, it set the standard for future philosophical and scientific writings in French. "The language of Descartes," writes Émile Boutroux, "is the fabric on which the style of our great writers is woven. Considered in itself, this language, stamped with the philosopher's method, possesses in the highest degree the noblest qualities of every language: propriety of terms, and the expression of order in ideas."[14]

The greatest of Descartes' works is his *Meditations on First Philosophy*, which first appeared in print in 1641, together with objections by such noted lights of the age as Thomas Hobbes, Pierre Gassendi, and Antoine Arnauld, and also Descartes' replies to them. In the *Meditations*, Descartes' ideas about human knowledge, God, and the distinction between body and mind, which first appeared in the *Discourse*, are given a more detailed and profound treatment. Descartes' third main work, *The Principles of Philosophy*, was published in 1644 in four books. In this he presents his entire philosophical system under separate articles in the manner of the college texts of the time. Descartes had hoped to spread his philosophy by having the *Principles* adopted as a text in the Jesuit schools, but his hope was not fulfilled. His last work, the *Passions of the Soul*, was written during the winter of 1645 but was not printed until 1649.

Descartes' stay in Holland for the most part was pleasant and uneventful, but in 1641 he became a center of controversy. It appears that the growing influence of Descartes' philosophy posed a threat to the professors who taught Aristotelean physics and cosmology at the Dutch universities. A dispute had arisen at the University of Utrecht between Henricus Regius, a professor of medicine who was a follower of Descartes, and Gesbert Voet, a theologian. On March 17, 1642, the senate of Utrecht prohibited the teaching of Descartes' philosophy, "first because it is new, next because it turns our youth away from the old, wholesome philosophy, and finally because it teaches various false and absurd opinions." Then in 1647 there came another attack on Descartes' philosophy, this time from the University of Leyden. The controversy became so bitter that Descartes, in order to defend himself from personal harm, had to 'seek protection from the French ambassador.

In 1648, disgusted by the controversy in Holland, Descartes accepted an invitation to become the tutor of Queen Christina of Sweden. Unfortunately, the queen demanded that he instruct her in philosophy at the unreasonable hour of five o'clock in the morning, when her mind, so she claimed, was most active. Returning from court one exceptionally cold February morning, Descartes contracted pneumonia from which he died a week later.

Thus, on February 11, 1650, at the age of fifty-four, died a man of whom Arthur Schopenhauer wrote:

Descartes is rightly deemed the father of modern philosophy, and this in a special, as well as a general sense, inasmuch as he placed the reason on its own feet by teaching men to use their own brains, in the place of which the Bible had previously served on the one hand, and Aristotle on the other. But in a more special and a narrower sense, he was this also; since he was the first to bring the problem upon which philosophy has mainly turned to consciousness—the problem of the Ideal and the Real—i.e., the question as to what in our knowledge is objective, and what is subjective; in other words, what might be ascribed by us to other things, and what we must ascribe to ourselves.[15]

Schopenhauer may be exaggerating, but it is at least a half-truth, and that is sufficient to place Descartes among the great thinkers of all time.

CHAPTER 2

The Regulae

ACCORDING to Descartes, arithmetic and geometry were the only sciences of his day which provided knowledge. No doubt there were propositions other than those of mathematics which Descartes was certain were true. He gives us examples of them: "what was once done can't be undone"; "I exist"; "every event has a cause." However, these propositions, unlike those of mathematics, are not members of an organized system of knowledge which constitutes a science. They are stray bits of knowledge without any logical connection with each other. Nor was Descartes, at this initial stage of his inquiry, denying that the propositions of the nonmathematical sciences of his day are true; they might possibly be true. The point he is making is that they are not known to be true. They are accepted, *unlike those in the mathematical sciences*, on inadequate grounds. But why, one might well ask, did Descartes believe that the mathematical sciences, and only those sciences, consisted of knowledge?

In Rule 2 of the *Regulae ad Directionem Ingenii* (*Rules for the Direction of the Mind*), Descartes writes, "Only those objects should engage our attention, to the sure and indubitable knowledge of which our mental powers seem to be adequate."[1] In this quotation, we have for the first time a statement of one of Descartes' most important doctrines—his insistence that knowledge, in the strict sense of the word, must be confined to beliefs which are indubitable. By "indubitable" Descartes does not mean merely the absence of doubt or the inability to doubt. For clearly, if a man honestly claims to know that the earth is a stationary body, then he is unable to doubt it. He does not, however, have knowledge, since what he believes is false. What Descartes means by a person's having indubitable knowl-

24

edge is that the person is aware that there could not possibly be, and not merely that there do not exist, grounds for doubting the truth of the proposition. It is not his mere inability to doubt, but his inability to doubt because he cannot conceive the possibility that he is mistaken. The man who claims to know that the earth is a stationary body can conceive the possibility that he is mistaken. He can imagine possible evidence which would make him change his mind. But what possible grounds could lead a person to give up his conviction that "a figure with three sides has three angles?" There are none. His belief is, therefore, a case of indubitable knowledge.

The nonmathematical sciences, according to Descartes, can at best provide only what is called "probable knowledge." He rejected the latter, because knowledge for him meant absolute security in belief. When a man knows that a proposition is true, he can rely on its truth without the slightest fear that he might possibly be mistaken. This security from falsehood can never apply to a probable belief, not even to one with a very high degree of probability. There cannot, therefore, be any probable knowledge. Probable knowledge, strictly speaking, was for Descartes a contradiction in terms. He writes, "Thus in accordance with the above maxim [the maxim of indubitable knowledge] we reject all such merely probable knowledge and make it a rule to trust only what is completely known and incapable of being doubted."[2] For Descartes, the clearest evidence that there is no knowledge in the nonmathematical sciences is the fact that there is scarcely a question—whether it be about the nature of the magnet or the behavior of the heavens—which is not an occasion for dispute, each philosopher proposing his favorite hypothesis:

For there is scarce any question occurring in the sciences about which talented men have not disagreed. But whenever two men come to opposite decisions about the same matter one of them at least must certainly be in the wrong, and apparently there is not even one of them who knows; for if the reasoning of the second was sound and clear he would be able so to lay it before the other as finally to succeed in convincing his understanding also. Hence apparently we cannot attain to a perfect knowledge in any such case of probable opinion, for it would be rashness to hope for more than others have attained to. *Consequently if we reckon correctly, of the sciences already discovered, Arithmetic and Geometry alone are left, to which the observance of this rule reduces us.*[3]

In Rule 2 Descartes gives his reason for believing that the mathematical sciences contain indubitable knowledge: "This furnishes us with an evident explanation of the great superiority in certitude of Arithmetic and Geometry to other sciences. The former alone deal with an object so pure and uncomplicated that they need make no assumptions at all which experience renders uncertain, but wholly consist in the rational deduction of consequences."[4] There is a danger here of misinterpreting Descartes. He is not claiming that the objects of the mathematical sciences are uncomplicated in the psychological sense that they are easy to understand. They are not. In the first place, there is a difficulty in bringing before the mind the purely abstract conceptions of a line and a point; and secondly, it is difficult to keep one's mind focused on them. They are uncomplicated only in the logical sense that their properties and relations are connected in such a manner that the mind can with ease move from one to another without the fear of possibly committing an error. For instance, when I keep the figure of a triangle before my mind, I can establish—by a step-by-step deduction—that the sum of its angles are equal to two right angles. In performing this task with care and attention, I am certain that no future experience could lead me to change my mind.

Having made the discovery that, to date, only the mathematical sciences provide indubitable knowledge, Descartes then proceeds to make the following recommendation:

But one conclusion now emerges out of those considerations, *viz*, not, indeed, that arithmetic and geometry are the sole sciences to be studied, but only that in our search for the direct road towards truth we should busy ourselves with no object which we cannot attain a certitude equal to that of the demonstrations of arithmetic and geometry.[5]

But might not Descartes have set his sights too high? There may after all be many matters about which we cannot achieve indubitable knowledge. If we accept Descartes' recommendation, and judge nothing to be true unless we have absolute certainty, we may have to settle for a very limited body of scientific knowledge. Descartes was aware of this criticism. In his answer he agreed that it is possible that there are many things about which we cannot know with any certainty. But this does not undermine the recommendation. Suppose we discover that with regard to a certain subject matter, human beings are unable, no matter how they try, to achieve indubitable knowledge. What have we lost? Nothing. What have we gained? The knowledge that this subject matter exceeds human intelligence, "For to have discovered this is knowledge in no less degree than the knowledge of anything else."[6]

Descartes not only recommended that we settle for nothing less for science than indubitable knowledge but also that we practice in the nonmathematical sciences the method of inquiry employed by the mathematicians. This recommendation is a revolutionary move and challenges the prevalent view of human knowledge. The Scholastics, who had dominated European thinking for four hundred years, under the influence of Aristotle, believed that different sciences require different methods and have different degrees of certainty. Aristotle in the *Nichomachean Ethics* is the authoritative spokesman for this position: "... it is the mark of an educated man to look for precision in each class of things just as far as the nature of the subject admits; it is evidently foolish to accept probable reasoning from a mathematician and to demand from a rhetorician scientific proofs."[7] The Aristotelean-Scholastic approach seems to be a sensible one. Why should anyone suppose that such radically different subjects as geometry and ethics require the identical method? Should not radical differences in subject matter dictate differences in method?

In Rule 1 of the *Regulae*[8] Descartes both criticizes the Aristotelean-Scholastic position and gives his reasons for believing that there is only one appropriate method for all the sciences. The Scholastic philosopher, says Descartes (he does not explicitly mention the Scholastic philosopher, but he no doubt had him in mind), distinguishes one science from another in the same manner as the arts are distinguished. The philosopher notices that the same man cannot acquire skill in all the arts, that the hands that become adept at agricultural tasks have consequently a difficulty in playing the harp. He then concludes that what is true of the arts is true of the sciences. They should be studied in isolation from each other, each with its appropriate method and with its own degree of certainty. "But this," writes Descartes, "is certainly wrong. For since the sciences taken all together are identical with human wisdom, which always remains one and the same, however applied to different subjects, and suffers no more differentiation proceeding from them than the light of the sun experiences from the variety of things which it illumines . . ."[9]

"Human wisdom" for Descartes means the proper employment of the intellect or, what amounts to the same thing, human intelligence: and the point he is making is that human intelligence is one. There is no one kind of intelligence, as the Scholastics would have us believe, appropriate for mathematics and another for ethics. In order to clarify his position, Descartes borrowed an analogy from Plato's *Republic*. Wisdom is like light. Light makes things visible and wisdom intelligible. And, just as there is no differentiation in the light of the sun because of the differences in the objects illuminated, so wisdom is not differentiated because of differences in subject matter. It is one and the same wisdom which renders intelligible such radically different objects as a mathematical figure, the human mind, the laws of motion, and the Almighty God. From the unity of wisdom, Descartes concluded that there can only be one appropriate method for all the sciences. That he would draw this conclusion is obvious, if one keeps in mind that for him, method consists of a set of rules for the correct employment of the intellect; it is nothing less than wisdom (that is, intelligence) in action.

Corresponding to Descartes' theme of the unity of human wisdom is his doctrine of the unity of science:

Hence we must believe that all the sciences are so inter-connected, that it is much easier to study them all together than to isolate one from all the others. If, therefore, anyone wishes to search out the truth of things in serious earnest, he ought not to select one special science; for all the sciences are conjoined with each other and interdependent . . .[10]

An example of this interdependence is to be found in Rule 8 of the *Regulae*, where Descartes deals with a problem in pure mathematics which requires for its solution considerations which belong to the science of physics. But, aside from this example and apart from his insistence that we employ mathematics in the solution of problems in the sciences of nature, the text of the *Regulae* is unhelpful in clarifying Descartes' conception of the unity of science. Fortunately, there is in Descartes' preface to the *Principles* a passage where he introduces his conception of the unity of the sciences in the image of a tree:

Thus philosophy [bear in mind that the term "philosophy" has a broader meaning than it has today] as a whole is like a tree whose roots are metaphysics, whose trunk is physics, and whose branches which issue from this trunk, are all the other sciences. These reduce themselves to three principal ones, *viz*, medicine, mechanics and morals . . .[11]

In the same work he speaks of the relationship between all the sciences as deductive. In order to understand what Descartes meant by this term, imagine a man who knows absolutely all the true propositions of all the sciences and wants to organize them in the most economical and systematic way. He would first introduce the propositions of metaphysics, that is, the existence of God and the ultimate nature of mind and matter, as his axioms. He would then deduce from them the theorems of physics and use the latter in turn as premises in order to derive propositions in medicine, mechanics, and morals. After he finished, he would possess a single large deductive system whose formal structure is analogous to Euclidean geometry. Descartes, on this interpretation, is not claiming that human beings will actually develop the sciences to the point that they can be organized into the form of a deductive model. The unity of science is an ideal which, though in principle is possible of attainment, may in fact never be realized.

In summary the following propositions constitute Descartes' rationalist ideal of science: (1) No proposition should be accepted in any science unless it is indubitably known to be true. (2) There is one method appropriate for all the sciences and that method is the one employed in the mathematical sciences. (3) The sciences are interconnected in such a manner as to form a single body of knowledge.

Descartes' ideal was to exert a great influence on later philosophers. Benedict de Spinoza, for instance, modeled his whole philosophical position on Euclidean geometry. The obvious question is whether Descartes, in developing his philosophical position, strictly adhered to the rationalist ideal. Did he practice what he preached? This is a matter that should be kept in mind as Descartes' philosophy is unfolded.

I *Intuition and Deduction*

Having presented his ideal of science, Descartes proceeds in Rule 3 to analyze the mental operations involved in the knowledge situation. There are, he claims, only two which can be relied on to give us knowledge without the fear of error. The two are intuition and deduction.

Descartes begins his discussion of intuition by informing us what it is not: "By *intuition* I understand, not the fluctuating testimony of the senses, nor the misleading judgment that proceeds from the blundering constructions of the imagination . . ."[12] In two respects, however, intuition resembles sense perception and imagination. First, all three involve a content which is immediately and directly inspected; secondly, the content in all three forms the basis for making judgments. By making a distinction between them Descartes wants to contrast the unreliability of sense perception and imagination with the reliability of intuition. Sense perception, he says, is subject to fluctuation. A perceptual experience varies with the conditions of the body and the medium of perception. For instance, my perceptual experience on the basis of which I am inclined to judge that there is a red spot on the wall depends on the lighting in the room, the condition of my sense organ, the state of my liver, and so on. I have no reason to be certain that my perceptual experience is an adequate basis for claiming that there is a red spot on the wall. For it is possible that at the present time the conditions of perception bring about a distortion in the sense content upon which I am inclined to base my judgment. We are even more prone to error when we rely on the imagination. The imagination, says Descartes, at times composes and connects things in an arbitrary manner. We have a tendency to judge that there are real connections between things merely because they are associated in our imagination. If, for instance, on a number of occasions I have witnessed the occurrence of a full moon, immediately followed by an epidemic, my imagination will form an association between the ideas of the two kinds of events. And, consequently, I may then be inclined to judge that there is a connection between the rise of the moon and the occurrence of an epidemic.

In contrast to sense perception and imagination, "intuition," writes Descartes, "is the undoubting conception of an unclouded and attentive mind, and springs from the light of reason alone..."[13] Here Descartes is attributing three characteristics to intuition. First, unlike sense perception and imagination, it is not possible for the mind to doubt what it intuits. Second, in order to have an intuition, the mind must be attentive and keep in clear focus the content under inspection. And third, intuition is a pure activity of the mind ("springs from the light of reason alone") which, unlike sense perception and imagination, is not dependent on the functions of the body. Only an entity, like a man, who is a fusion of body and mind, could have sense perception and imagination as well as intuition. A disembodied angel, for instance, could only have intuitions.

Descartes presents some examples of intuitions: "Thus each individual can mentally have an intuition of the fact that he exists, and that he thinks; that the triangle is bounded by three lines only, the sphere by a single superficies, and so on."[14] It is apparent from these examples that Descartes considers intuition to be a mental perception of a propositional content which the mind cannot withhold judging to be true. His examples fall into either of two categories. The first are necessary truths, which are about facts that could not possibly have been otherwise, like 2 and 2 make 4, and whatever has a figure is extended. The other category consists of propositions about the existence and the states of one's own mind at the time when

they occur, such as "I intend to leave the room," or "I hope
that Jones is well." The latter are not necessary truths; for, while
true, they might possibly have been false. It is possible that I
might never have been born; and though I am alive, I need
not necessarily have the thoughts or desires that I am at
present experiencing.

But clearly, if knowledge was confined to the kind of immediate and direct intuitions illustrated above, scientific knowledge would not be possible. We would have nothing but stray
bits of knowledge without any systematic coherence between
them. We could not then have any science. There must therefore, besides intuition, be a supplementary way of knowing;
this supplementary way Descartes called "deduction." Deduction
is not the source of a special kind of knowledge, distinct from
intuition. It is rather, as Norman Kemp Smith says, "the process
by which intuition extends itself so as to take in what at first
appears to exceed its grasp."[15] Deduction, according to Descartes,
is a movement of the mind which consists in a sequence of
intuitions where the intuition of some members depends on
the mind's having intuited previous ones. Consider the following
example. In order to have an intuition that $2 + 2 = 3 + 1$, I
first have to "see" intuitively that $2 + 2 = 4$ and likewise "see"
that $3 + 1 = 4$. Then I intuit that the former proposition is a
necessary consequence of the latter two. What is central to
deduction is that, if I had merely considered by itself that
$2 + 2 = 3 + 1$, I could not possibly have intuited it to be a
fact. It is only because my mind first intuited each of the
other two propositions that I could no longer doubt that
$2 + 2 = 3 + 1$. Descartes on this point is explicit and clear:

Hence now we are in a position to raise the question as to why
we have, besides intuition, given this supplementary method of
knowing, viz, knowing by deduction, by which we understand all
necessary inference from other facts that are known with certainty.
This, however, we could not avoid, because many things are known
with certainty, though not by themselves evident, but only deduced
from true and known principles by the continuous and uninterrupted
action of a mind that has a clear vision of each step in the process.[16]

It is apparent from what has been said that intuited propositions can be divided into two classes. Those which can be intuited without the need of deduction and those which cannot. The former we shall call "self-evident truths" and the latter "mediated intuitions." They differ, according to Descartes, in two respects. Mediated intuitions require, in order to be known, a certain movement of the mind. This is not true of self-evident truths. Second, mediated intuitions, unlike self-evident truths, depend for their certainty on memory. Descartes was concerned about this matter as it pertained to long chains of reasoning, because he realized that memory is not always reliable. One of the rules of method called "enumeration," which we shall consider later, was introduced specifically to limit a person's need to rely on memory where long deductions are necessary.

Descartes contrasts his conception of deduction from that of syllogistic reasoning. In the latter case, an inference from $2 + 2 = 4$ and $3 + 1 = 4$ to $2 + 2 = 3 + 1$ requires as a premise the universal proposition that things which are equal to the same thing are equal to each other. But in Descartes' conception of deduction, no such premise is needed. On the contrary, it is from such deduction as $2 + 2 = 3 + 1$ because $2 + 2 = 4$ and $3 + 1 = 4$ that we intuit the universal proposition that things equal to the same thing are equal to each other. To Claude Clerselier Descartes writes:

The most considerable error is that this writer [Gassendi] supposes that the knowledge of particular propositions should always be deduced from universal propositions, following the order of the syllogisms of the Dialectic. In all this matter, he shows that he knows very little about the way which truth should be sought. For it is certain that, in order to discover truth, we should always begin with particular notions in order to reach general notions afterwards, though reciprocally, after having discovered the general notions, we may deduce from them others which are particular.[17]

The other objection which Descartes raised against the syllogism, and for that matter against formal reasoning in general, is that it is useless for the purpose of discovering new knowledge. The conclusion of the syllogism must already be known to be true prior to the person's inferring it from the premises. For instance, take the standard example of a syllogism: All men are mortal; Socrates is a man; hence, Socrates is mortal. Now, in order to know that the premise that all men are mortal is true, I must already know the conclusion that Socrates is mortal, since I know that he is a man. Descartes claimed that his conception of deduction is a mental activity by which new knowledge is acquired; whereas the syllogism has a use only in arranging what is already known for the purpose of teaching.

II *Rules of Method*

Intuition and deduction are not rules of method, but the natural ways by which the mind comes to know things. On the other hand, the rules of method are strategies for best utilizing intuition and deduction for the resolution of problems and the achievement of a unified system of scientific knowledge. They perform two other tasks. It is by employing the rules that a man can guard himself against error. This point is clearly brought out in an encounter between Gassendi and Descartes. In the fifth set of objections Gassendi points out that there are many and varied opinions among men; each thinks that he perceives clearly and distinctly the belief which he holds (clarity and distinctness is Descartes' criterion of truth). What Descartes needs, writes Gassendi, is a method by which a person can distinguish his merely seeming to have a clear and distinct perception from his actually having one.[18] Descartes' answer is: "But I contend that this has been carefully attended to in its proper place...."[19] Descartes' method is precisely what Gassendi was asking him to provide, and Descartes merely referred him to the *Meditations*, where he had employed his method in order to discover the first principles of knowledge. Another use of the method is that it enables us to "determine the nature and scope of human knowledge." Descartes held that there is nothing more wasteful and pointless than disputes about the secrets of nature, the influence of the heavens on the earth, and similar matters without men having first inquired whether human reason is adequate for these tasks.[20] But, in order to make this inquiry, we require a right method for the pursuit of knowledge, which, when applied to some subject, will enable us either to discover the truth or learn that, in this particular area, knowledge is not possible, for the subject exceeds the powers of the human understanding. The matter just stated is summarized by Descartes in Rule 4 of the *Regulae*: " ... by a method I mean certain and simple rules, such that, if a man observe them accurately, he shall never assume what is false as true, and will never spend his mental efforts to no purpose, but will always gradually increase his knowledge and so arrive at a true understanding of all that does not surpass his powers."[21]

There are a number of significant characteristics of Descartes' rules of method. First, Descartes' method does not contain logical rules by which a person, applying them in a mechanical way, can distinguish truth from error. Two people may read Descartes' rules, understand them, apply them to the same subject matter; one will achieve knowledge, whereas the other, through lack of skill in applying the method, will not. This fact about Descartes' method bothered Gottfried Leibniz, who demanded of method that it be "palpable" and "mechanical."[22] Second, Descartes' rules apply to all subjects: to mathematics as well as to ethics. Descartes, however, wisely realized that, if his rules are to be the same, regardless of differences in subject matter, they have to be somewhat open-textured and not detailed and specific. He does not, for example, in his geometry, appear to use the same method as he does in the *Meditations*, although he would claim that he does. He would insist that there are not two different methods but only differences in application. For instance, in metaphysics, the problem of eliminating prejudiced and unfounded beliefs is central; it is not so in mathematics. In mathematics, the imagination is a useful aid; in metaphysics, it is a hindrance. Because of this open-textured nature of the rules and their universal applicability, Descartes thought of them as rules for the right use of human intelligence. They are nothing less than a description of what it is to be a rational person. Third, people are not born with the knowledge or the ability to use the method, nor like walking, do they automatically acquire it at some later stage in life. The ability to use the rules is a skill which a person can only acquire by applying it to some subject matter. Descartes suggests that he first apply it to the mathematical sciences because it is much easier to apply it there since former bad habits of thinking are less prone to deflect his mind from the right way in that area. Once he has succeeded in developing the skill in mathematics, he can then apply the rules to more difficult subjects. Finally, the rules contain both psychological and logical elements. That it contains the former is due to the fact that Descartes' method was not intended to be a set of rules for demonstrating the truths of propositions but a vehicle for discovering new truths. The stress is not on proof but on discovery. Therefore, Descartes' method involves advice to get rid of one's prejudices, train oneself to concentrate one's mind on one thing at a time, and so on.

Descartes' rules of method are found both in the *Regulae* and in the *Discourse*. The first rule in the *Discourse* summarizes a number of rules in the *Regulae*: "To accept nothing as true which I did not clearly recognize to be so: that is to say, carefully to avoid precipitation and prejudice in judgments, and to accept in them nothing more than what was present to my mind so clearly and distinctly that I could have no occasion to doubt it."[23]

The next section will deal with clarity and distinctness. At present, something needs to be said about the other aspect of the rule, which is "To avoid precipitation and prejudice in judgments." A prejudice is a belief which is accepted as true without being known to be true. To avoid error, a person must learn how to guard himself from accepting prejudices. But, in order to achieve this knowledge, he should first acquaint himself with the causes of prejudices. The first and foremost cause is that as children we accept things at face value. Since the earth does not feel as if it were moving, the child concludes that it is stationary. Second, as children, and even later in life, we have a tendency to rely on authorities, parents, teachers, and custom. Still another cause of prejudice and error rests on the fact that we have to use language in order to express our thoughts. Through constant usage, the connection between words and thoughts become so close that often, in using words, we are deceived into thinking that we are expressing thoughts when we are not. A source of prejudice reserved exclusively to the learned is their love of dealing with obscure matters. They confuse the obscure with the profound. Throughout the *Regulae* there is advice on how to overcome these prejudices. For instance, in Rule 9,[24] as against the learned, Descartes says that, if we wish to understand how one and the same cause can produce contrary effects, we should not bother to consult such obscure subjects as medicine and astrology but consider a balance in which the same weight raises one arm at the same time as it depresses the other. The most celebrated example of how a person should go about trying to free himself from all prejudices occurs in the *First Meditation* where Descartes attempts to adopt a skeptical attitude toward all his beliefs.

The second and third rules of method in the *Discourse* are called "the rule of analysis" and "the rule of synthesis," respectively. The rule of analysis is: "... to divide up each of the difficulties which I examined into as many parts as possible, and as seemed requisite in order that it might be resolved in the best manner possible."[25] And the rule of synthesis is:

... to carry on my reflections in due order, commencing with objects that were the most simple and easy to understand, in order to rise little by little, or by degrees, to knowledge the most complex, assuming an order, even if a fictitious one, among those which do not follow a natural sequence relatively to one another.[26]

These two rules appear in the *Regulae* as Rule 5:

Method consists in the order and disposition of the objects towards which our mental vision must be directed if we would find out any truth. We shall comply with it exactly if we reduce involved and obscure propositions step by step to those that are simpler, and then starting with the intuitive apprehension of all those that are absolutely simple, attempt to ascend to the knowledge of all others by precisely similar steps.[27]

Descartes' rules cannot be appreciated from the mere consideration of the abstract and general formulation presented above. Descartes was well aware of this fact and therefore published the *Discourse* together with works on optics and meteors, as well as a work on geometry, to show how he employed these rules successfully to make discoveries in pure mathematics as well as in physics. This action confirms the point previously made that the rules cannot be specific and detailed if they are to apply to all subjects. In consideration of this matter, the rules may be illustrated by an example found in Rule 8 of the *Regulae*.[28] Suppose a pure mathematician sets out to determine that curve from which parallel rays are refracted in such a manner that they afterward meet at a point. Now, in accordance with the rule of analysis, he will at once see that the determination of this line depends on the relation which the angles of refraction bear to the angles of incidence. But he will also note that, in order to determine this latter fact, he requires a knowledge of physics. If he then wishes to discover the truth and does not simply confine his work to pure mathematics, the inquirer will discover that the ratio between the angles of incidence and the angles of refraction depends on changes in their relation produced by varying the medium. These changes in turn depend on the manner in which the ray of light penetrates the whole body. Further, it will become apparent that this manner of penetration presupposes a knowledge of the nature of light. Finally, he will find that knowledge of the latter depends on knowledge of what a natural power is in general. With this last term in his investigation, he will have reached the most simple link in the series. He can then, in accordance with the rule of synthesis, return step by step in the complete implicative series.

Comprehending, or rendering intelligible, any phenomenon for Descartes involves the analysis of a complex into its simple constituents through a systematic reduction and then reversing the order. We should not, writes Descartes, in trying to understand why a magnet attracts bodies, introduce some mysterious occult property in the magnet. We ought rather to collect all the observations which we can muster about the magnet and from these, applying the rule of analysis, attempt to deduce the simple elements of which the magnet is composed and which it has to possess in a certain combination in order to produce those effects which we observe in the behavior of the magnet.[29]

The ultimate limit of reductive analysis is what in the *Regulae*

Descartes calls "a simple nature." Descartes explains what he means by this latter term by citing an example. A body has both extension and figure. It is not, however, literally compounded of corporeal nature, extension, and figure, since these elements have never existed in isolation from each other. It is only relative to our understanding that we call it a compound constructed out of these three natures, since we have thought of them separately before we were able to judge that the three were found in one and the same subject. Now we can analyze body into extension and figure, but we cannot analyze figure and extension into simpler elements without generating confusion. Consequently, in this matter, figure and extension are the ultimate atoms of analysis and are called "simple natures."[30]

Simple natures, Descartes goes on to inform us, are divided into three classes. They are either purely intellectual or purely material, or else common to both intellect and to matter. Those which are purely intellectual are apprehended by our understanding by means of a certain "inborn light" without the aid of the senses or the imagination. Examples are what knowing is, what doubt is, what ignorance is, what volition is, and so on. We have knowledge of these things despite the fact that we cannot form an image of any of them. Then there are those things which are purely material and which we detect only in bodies, that is, figure, extension, motion, etc. And, finally, there are those which apply to both corporeal and spiritual things, that is, existence, unity, duration, and the like. Besides simple natures, there are "common notions," which are, as it were, bonds connecting simple natures and constituting the basis for all reasoning. These common notions can be discovered either by the intellect alone or by it in conjunction with images of material things. Descartes gives two examples of common notions: "Things that are the same as a third thing are the same as one another"; "Things which do not bear the same relation to a third thing have some diversity from each other."[31]

We cannot be mistaken regarding these simple natures. "...We assert that all these simple natures are known *per se* and are wholly free from falsity," declares Descartes.[32] Since a nature is simple, to think of it at all is to think of it completely; consequently, we cannot confuse it with something else. To use the technical language of Descartes, it is not only clear but distinct. Now since all composite things are made up of simple natures, it follows that, in order to have an adequate rational understanding of any phenomenon whatsoever, we must intuit the simple natures out of which it is composed and the precise manner in which they are combined: ". . . No knowledge is at any time possible of anything beyond these simple natures and what may be called their intermixture and combination with each other."[33]

Descartes' doctrine of "simple natures" is not mentioned in his later works. The obvious question is, did Descartes abandon his theory by 1637 or retain it without specifying it? The answer, I believe, depends on how Descartes' theory is to be correctly interpreted. On one interpretation, Descartes held that simple natures are entities which might conceivably have existed in isolation from each other or in combinations other than those that in fact prevail. Simple natures, on this interpretation, are substances. This position is clearly inconsistent with Decartes' doctrine of "true and immutable essences" and with his theory of substance, both of which are to be found in his *Meditations* and *Principles*. On another, and I believe correct, interpretation, the theory of simple natures is not inconsistent with his later work. The simple natures, on this interpretation, are not, as L. J. Beck points out, to be thought of as atoms of reality: "The simple natures enclose and engender a number of relations which may be of an infinite complexity, the total constituting the whole of reality and the whole of knowledge."[34] On this interpretation, I do not intuit a simple nature without intuiting it as necessarily implicated with something else. I do not, for instance, intuit figure, then intuit extension, and then a relation between them. There are not three intuitions involved here. Rather, in intuiting figure in a distinct unconfused manner by which its total nature is luminous to my mind, I intuit that it is necessarily implicated with extension, in the sense that nothing could conceivably exist which has a figure and is not extended. The reason for the fact that there is in this case a single intuition is that the relation between the two is internal in the sense that it is an essential aspect of the nature of a figure to be a mode of extension. The simplicity of the simple natures does not mean that they have no relations but only that they stand in no relation by virtue of a part or aspect of themselves but only by virtue of their total nature. I, for instance, stand in the spatial relation of being to the left of Peter by virtue of the corporeal aspect of myself, but not by virtue of what I am as a thinking entity. On the other hand, I stand in the relation to God as creature to creator by virtue of my total being. The interpretation of the theory of simple natures which I have just enunciated is not contrary to Descartes' later works.

The methods of analysis and synthesis reveal Descartes' conception of the nature of an adequate explanation, that is to say, what it is to understand something or to render something intelligible. For Descartes, it is to detect a set of necessary implications between the elements of the phenomena that have to be explained and the principles involved in their composition. Descartes' conception of explanation is broadly mechanistic. I call it "mechanistic," not because of the kind of phenomena which it explains, but because of its form. The mechanistic form of explanation applies not only to bodies but to minds, not only to substances but to abstract studies (mathematics) as well. This Cartesian approach to what constitutes an adequate explanation is a radical departure from that of Aristotle and his medieval followers. Their primary form of explanation was teleological. It was based on the notion that every individual in nature is a member of a species or kind, which, by virtue of its formal essence, has a certain *telos*, or goal, the knowledge of which can be used for the purpose of explaining the processes that the individuals undergo. Thus, a stone, when released, falls to the surface of the earth because, being a solid, its natural place is to be in a state of rest on the surface of the earth. A vegetable, for instance, by virtue of its form, which is the vegetable soul, undergoes the organic processes of growth, nutrition, and reproduction. Descartes' position is that attempts at explaining natural processes teleologically are worthless, because they rest on a confused and obscure conception of nature.

The fourth and last rule of method in the *Discourse* is the rule of enumeration, which is "in all cases to make enumerations so complete and reviews so general that I should be certain of having omitted nothing." This rule is introduced in order to deal with cases of deduction where it is not possible for the intellect to have an intuition of all the steps in the deduction, because there are far too many of them. For example, suppose we have the following progression, A, B, C, D, E. A is intuited and so is the step from A to B and from B to C, and so on. Yet the conclusion that there is a necessary connection between A and E by means of the intermediate steps in the deductive progression is not present to our mental vision with the certainty of intuition. The length of the chain of deduction in this case exceeds the scope of our intuitive power. We have, therefore, to rely on memory; but unfortunately, memory is not always reliable. Consequently, in the strict sense of the term "know," in a long chain of deduction the conclusion is not known to be true, since there is always the possibility that one link in the deductive chain is missing and, through faulty memory, we may not apprehend its absence.

In order to meet this difficulty, Descartes introduced the rule of enumeration. What he advised is that we continuously go over the steps of the proof so that we are able to perform the deduction with greater rapidity, thus minimizing the role of memory, for the purpose of intuiting all the steps in the deduction simultaneously. In the *Regulae* he writes:

Thus if diverse mental acts have led me to know what is the relation between a first and a second magnitude, next between the second and the third, then between the third and fourth, and finally the fourth and a fifth, that need not lead me to see what is the relation between the first and the fifth, nor can I deduce it from what I already know, unless I remember all the other relations. Hence what I have to do is to run over them all repeatedly in my mind, until I pass so quickly from the first to the last that practically no step is left to the memory, and I seem to view the whole all at the same time.[35]

Despite the employment of the rule of enumeration for the purpose of limiting our reliance on memory, we will at times still have to accept long chains of reasoning, where all the steps cannot be brought under an intuition. One of Descartes' concerns, which raised a serious problem for him in the *Meditations*, is that in the development of a science, given the limits of human cognitive powers, we shall have to accept conclusions where all the justifying steps in the argument cannot be intuited at the same time.

III   *Clear and Distinct Perception*

Descartes' criterion of knowledge is embodied in the rule that "whatever is clearly and distinctly perceived is true." In order to understand this rule, we must first consider his use of the term "idea" and the significance of ideas in his theory of knowledge. Unfortunately, Descartes is not always consistent in his use of the term. Professor Anthony Kenny is correct when he says, "Sometimes . . . an idea is [for Descartes] an operation or act of the mind; at other times it is not so much an act of the mind as the object or content of such an act."[36] Descartes' explicit statements regarding his use of the term is that it is to be regarded as an object. Thus, in one of his replies to the third set of objections, he writes: "I take the term 'idea' to stand for whatever the mind directly perceives . . ."[37] According to this definition we would have to rank as ideas concepts such as those of God or of a triangle, sensations such as heat and pain, as well as images, since they are all directly perceived. Descartes, however, did not hold the position which Locke was to maintain, namely, that the only things that the mind directly perceives are its own contents. On the contrary, according to Descartes, when we visually perceive things or remember past events, or dream, there are present before our minds physical images which are located in a part of the brain. They are not, however, physical bodies but are rather like mirror images and shadows, mere physical phenomena. Despite the above, Descartes has to be classified, with Locke, as a representationalist in that he believed that no person could directly perceive bodies—not even his own—and that the only way a person can acquire knowledge of the physical world and other minds is by means of ideas which he directly perceives. "I am certain," Descartes writes to Gibieuf, "that I can have no knowledge of what is outside me except by means of ideas within me . . ."[38] Given this position, Descartes has to devise some way by which a person's direct inspection of his ideas can reveal to him what is true or false. Clarity and distinctness in perception is the criterion (together with his method) for accomplishing this task.

In the *Regulae*, Descartes does not define clear and distinct perception, but he does so in the *Principles*:

I term that clear which is present and apparent to an attentive mind, in the same way as we assert that we see objects clearly when, being present to the regarding eye, they operate upon it with sufficient strength. But the distinct is that which is so precise and different from all other objects that it contains within itself nothing but what is clear.[39]

Descartes then gives us an example of how a perception can be clear but not distinct:

When, for instance, a severe pain is felt, the perception of this pain may be very clear, and yet for all that, not distinct, because it is usually confused by the sufferers with the obscure judgment that they form upon its nature, assuming as they do that something exists in the part affected, similar to the sensation of pain of which they are alone clearly conscious. In this way perception may be clear without being distinct, and cannot be distinct without being also clear.[40]

What is the object of the clear and distinct perception? Is it the feeling of pain? No. Descartes claims that what is clearly and distinctly perceived is true and that the feeling of pain is not the kind of thing for which the terms "true" and "false" apply. The most likely candidate for what the sufferer clearly perceived is the proposition "I am in pain." This is so for two reasons. First, propositions are used by Descartes to illustrate clear and distinct perception. In the *Second Meditation*, for instance, he claims that he clearly and distinctly perceives that he is a thinking thing.[41] Second, Descartes assigns the terms "true" and "false" to propositions. Granted that it is only judgments which are true (that is, formally true) in the strict sense of the word, propositions and concepts, however, have what he calls "material truth." The proposition, "Socrates is wise" is true if, in fact, Socrates is wise; and Descartes' concept of a material body is true if material bodies actually have the characteristics which make up Descartes' concept of a body.

While there is a distinction between the feeling of pain and the proposition, "I am in pain," they are, nevertheless, very closely connected. The proposition is "clear" because the feeling of pain makes the truth of the proposition evident. The proposition in Descartes' example is, however, not perceived "distinctly" because the sufferer assumes that the fact that he is in pain entails that there is something going on in his body which resembles the pain. His assumption is false. The feeling of pain constitutes sufficient grounds for the former but not for the latter. The sufferer has failed to distinguish what he cannot doubt on the basis of the evidence available to him, namely, his having a sensation of pain from what he can doubt, that is, that something was going on in his body which resembled the sensation. He has failed to distinguish in this case what is clear to him from what is not. We may generalize from the above example. A person "clearly" perceives a proposition to be true if he cannot possibly doubt its truth on the basis of available evidence; he perceives it "distinctly" if he draws no inferences from the proposition that are not strictly warranted by the evidence.

Descartes also speaks of concepts (ideas) as being clear and distinct. This is not a different conception of clarity and distinctness from the one just presented. This fact is apparent if one bears in mind that the explication of a concept consists in propositions. If I am asked what my concept of a square is, I will answer: "A square is a four-sided figure"; "the angles of a square are all equal"; and so on. The latter are propositions.

Descartes gives us examples of clear and distinct ideas and of confused and obscure ones. The Christian has a clear and distinct idea of God insofar as he has a conception of an eternal, omniscient, omnipotent being and does not attribute to God any property that is incompatible with his perfection. The idolator, on the other hand, has a confused conception of God, because he includes in his idea such logically incompatible attributes as being perfect and being vindictive. Again, a clear conception of a body is that of a substance which is extended, moveable, and flexible. The atomists, on the other hand, have a confused concept, since they attribute to an atom two incompatible properties, namely, occupying space and being indivisible.[42]

Clarity and distinctness also admit of degrees. Once an idea has the minimum of clearness and distinctness, it can become clearer and more distinct. For instance, a person ignorant of geometry may have a clear idea of the nature of a triangle, in the sense that he understands it to be a figure comprehended by three lines and distinct in that he does not attribute to it any properties which are not necessarily implicated in the above specification of its nature. But the clarity of that idea is at a minimum. As he studies geometry, there is a constant increase in the clarity of that idea, for he begins to intuit a necessary connection between a figure comprehended by three sides and other properties, such as that its greatest side is subtended by the greatest angle and that the three angles are equal to two right angles, and so on. The clearer his idea becomes, the more distinct it is, because the more properties he learns that belong to a triangle, the better he is able to distinguish it from other figures. The mathematician's conception of a triangle is what Descartes, in his later works, calls "a true and immutable nature." Professor Alan Gewirth describes it in the following way:

But once thus constituted as a direct object of perception, an idea of the latter sort [a true and immutable nature] is, with regard to its further significance, an independent logical entity containing within itself a system of implications, of simple natures and their relations, which deduction may gradually reveal, and which indeed it is the task of science progressively to discover.[43]

IV *Sense and Imagination*

In the *Regulae*, Descartes assigns an important role to the faculties of sense and imagination in the acquisition of knowledge. In the *Meditations*, however, he considers them a hindrance. The two seemingly conflicting positions can be reconciled by considering the place of the faculties of sense and imagination in Descartes' theory of knowledge.

What does Descartes mean by a faculty, and how are faculties to be distinguished? A common misinterpretation is to attribute to Descartes the position that what distinguishes one faculty from another is a difference in the mode of perception; that, for instance, seeing a man walking down the street, and "seeing" that the angles of a square are all right angles, are different ways of perceiving something. Not at all, says Descartes; the mode of perception is the same. Both are activities of the understanding. Where they differ is in the objects perceived. In the case of imagination and sense perception, the understanding considers either the images which are patterns in the brain or the mental states brought about because of the mind's close intimacy with the body; whereas, in intellectual vision it considers itself, that is, the contents of the mind, insofar as it does not rely on the body.[44] In a letter to Mersenne, Descartes writes, "The mind acquires all of its knowledge by the reflection it makes, either on itself in respect to things which are mental, or on the diverse dispositions of the brain to which it is joined for the things which are corporeal."[45]

In the first three *Meditations*, Descartes constantly reminds himself that he must not give in to his natural tendency of relying on his senses as a source of knowledge: "I shall now close my eyes, I shall stop my ears, I shall call away all my senses, I shall efface even from my thoughts all the images of corporeal things, or at least (for that is hardly possible) I shall esteem them as vain and false; and thus holding converse only with myself and considering my own nature, I shall try little by little to reach a better knowledge of and a more familiar acquaintanceship with myself."[46] One should not conclude from this passage that Descartes is condemning the senses as a source of scientific knowledge, but should bear in mind that the *Meditations* is a treatise on first philosophy, that is, the principles upon which all the sciences ultimately depend. In the above passage, Descartes is expressing his position that in metaphysics we should eschew any reliance on the senses or the imagination. He is not necessarily implying that his recommendation for metaphysics should be adopted for the other sciences as well.

But why did Descartes consider sense and imagination a hindrance to metaphysical knowledge? He gives his answer in a reply to the second set of objections.[47] Asked by a critic why he began his *Meditations* with skepticism rather than with axioms and postulates in the manner of geometry, he answered (in part) that, while the axioms and postulates of geometry are acquired from the pure activity of the understanding, they harmonize with our sense experiences, as is apparent from the fact that the senses and the imagination are aids in the study of geometry. But the matter is different in the case of metaphysics; for while its primary principles are as intelligible as those of geometry, they do not, however, agree with the senses. In order, therefore, to pursue metaphysical truth, the mind must begin by turning away from the senses and the imagination and must, so to speak, fall back on the understanding alone, which for Descartes is the mind when freed from its intimate association with the body. This act of turning away from the senses and the imagination can be accomplished only by adopting a skeptical attitude toward all of one's beliefs. Descartes realized here that if he did not suspend his reliance on the senses and the imagination, he could not articulate a conception of himself as a distinctly thinking being which he held to be the principle lying at the foundation of all the sciences.

Sense experience can also be a barrier in the acquisition of knowledge in the science of nature. But, here, unlike in metaphysics, it is not the use of the senses and the imagination but their uncritical employment that is the barrier. Human beings are born with a natural tendency, which they exercise from earliest childhood, to think of corporeal bodies as resembling the immediate objects of the senses. Consequently, they believe that bodies possess color, smell, and heat exactly as we experience them and that changes in the physical world are qualitative as well as quantitative. But to think of the world in this manner is to make it impossible to develop a science of nature which is both fully intelligible and also useful for transforming nature for human purposes. The principles of such a science should be expressed in mathematical equations. This method at once excludes color and sound as properties of bodies. For, as Descartes writes in the *Regulae*:

Though one thing can be said to be more or less white, than another, or a sound sharper or flatter, and so on, it is yet impossible to determine exactly whether greater exceeds the less in the proportion two to one, or three to one, etc., unless we treat the quantity as being in a certain way analogous to the extension of a body possessing figure. Let us then take it as fixed and certain that perfectly definite "questions" are almost free from difficulty other than that of transmuting ratios, so that they may be stated as equations.[48]

Despite the above recommendations, the senses for Descartes have a significant and indispensable role to play in developing the science of nature. In the first place, our first awareness of the ideas of extension and motion is the result of sense experience.[49] Second, the knowledge of the existence of physical bodies would not be possible without our having sense experience. And third, sense experience plays an important role in developing the science of nature. This last matter requires some commentary.

In the science of nature Descartes distinguished universal physics from such sciences as physiology, mechanics, and astronomy. He believed that the propositions of universal physics are deducible from certain propositions in metaphysics. For instance, the principle that the quantity of motion in the world is constant is deducible from the fact that God, who is always consistent and economical in his ways, first initiated motion in the world. Sense experience, while not necessary in developing universal physics, may nevertheless play a useful role. Observations may suggest the problems from which the deductive process of thinking starts, and experiments can be used to test the principles that were already established on *a priori* grounds. As mentioned previously, universal physics is not all of the science of nature. Universal physics establishes that the world is a mechanistic system and a few basic, very general principles; but the detailed aspects of nature, the distribution of the stars, the behavior of the tides, and so on, cannot be deduced from the propositions of universal physics. In their case, sense experience is not merely useful but necessarily indispensable. An excellent statement of this position is given by James Collins:

At this point, we must catch the epistemological significance of Descartes' prime distinction between the *general* meanings of nature and the *progressively more determinate* meanings oriented toward our experienced world. Even after we are able to develop a complex general significance for nature in terms of God, material particles, and the laws of movement, we are not in possession of a fully satisfactory concept of nature. For this complex general sense of nature is not terminal, but instrumental, in our continuing study of experienced natural reality. The concepts of nature must be rendered constantly more determinate and concrete. This requires us to seek an ever closer continuity between the general meaning and the more particularized study of the appearing world, the human environment of our earth and the kinds of bodies we encounter and use.[50]

Leibniz's concept of an infinite number of possible universes is helpful here. Given an infinite number of possible universes, which have extension and motion, each of them will constitute a mechanistic system with a determinate number of types of particles which behave in accordance with a few simple laws. But these principles of general physics cannot explain the detailed facts observed in nature, for these facts will be true of some universes with extension and motion but not true of others. They cannot, for instance, account for the complex mechanisms of animal bodies, for the existence of such mechanisms belongs to our universe but is not true of other possible physical universes. What universal physics does is to restrict the kinds of acceptable explanations and sets a theoretical limit to the kinds of properties that are permitted in subsidiary and more concretely specific inquiries.

Given the above, it is apparent that observation and experiment are indispensable in the study of nature at a more specific and detailed level. Careful observations have to be made in order to locate and articulate a problem and experiments employed in order to compare explanatory hypotheses for the purpose of choosing the most plausible one:

As I have to confess [writes Descartes], the power of nature is so ample, so vast, and these principles [the principles of general physics] so simple and so general, that of the particular effects, there is hardly one that I do not recognize as allowing of being accounted for in several different ways, and usually my greatest difficulty is to discover in which of these various ways it has to be viewed. . . . Accordingly, my progress in the knowledge of nature will be greater or less, according as I shall have the means of making more or fewer observations.[51]

We shall be fortunate if we can discover a hypothesis which can explain the facts which led us to pose the problem. But, as Descartes points out, strictly speaking we cannot know that such a causal account is true, for there are a number of contrary accounts which could also possibly explain the facts.

It is worth remarking that, despite the rationalistic and mathematical orientation of Descartes' thinking, his position with regard to the detailed studies of nature was empirical in tone; and the fact that he refused to label the conclusions in such inquiries as knowledge does not alter the fact that he had a less ambitious view of the capacities and possibilities of human knowledge than the many rationalist thinkers who were inspired by him. Descartes did not remain true to that rationalist ideal which he so eloquently stated; but in this matter his good sense was stronger than his rationalistic vision.

V *The Search for a First Principle*

The term "metaphysics" has been used occasionally in this chapter without explaining what Descartes meant by it. Descartes' use of the term differs from that of the Scholastics. The latter, following Aristotle, meant by "metaphysics" the science of being *qua* being, that is, the science which studies what must be true of everything that exists. For instance, the statement that "the same thing cannot both be and not be at the same time" is a metaphysical principle for the Scholastics because it applies to everything that exists. They also used the term to signify a study of the noblest and the first in the order of being, namely, that science that concerns itself with the existence and attributes of God. God is that entity upon whom all things without exception depend for their existence. The Scholastic orientation to the sciences was from the standpoint of the objects of inquiry. That is why they adopted different methods for different subject matter. Descartes, on the other hand, made the problem of knowledge central to his philosophical enterprise; consequently his orientation toward the sciences was from the point of view of the agent. As a result of this shift in perspective, Descartes found a new use for the old term "metaphysics." It was to become the science of the first principles of knowledge, that is, the first things a person discovers to exist when he reasons in a scientific and methodical manner. Metaphysics begins with an attempt to discover the *first* principle.

The first principle, according to Descartes, is a proposition which has the following four characteristics: (1) it is either a self-evident truth or one deducible from a self-evident truth in one or two steps; (2) it is about an actual existent entity and not a hypothetical one; (3) the knowledge of its truth does not presuppose the existence of anything else; and (4) it is what logicians call deductively fruitful in the sense that it is possible to derive other truths from it. On this matter Descartes, in a letter to Clerselier, writes: "I will also add that one should not require the first principle to be such that all other propositions can be reduced to it and proved by it. It is enough if it is useful for the discovery of many and if there is no other proposition on which it depends, and none which is easier to discover."[52]

Neither mathematics nor the science of nature can, according to Descartes, provide us with the first principle. The mathematical sciences treat existence hypothetically. For example, from the true proposition "equilateral triangles are equiangular," I cannot infer that there exist equilateral triangles. While the above statement in pure geometry is categorical grammatically, its logical status is hypothetical and should read, "If something were an equilateral triangle, then it would be equiangular." In this respect, Descartes differs from Plato. For Plato, the above statement is a logically categorical proposition about the relation between two abstract entities. Plato believed that mathematical entities exist; that, besides the concrete triangular bodies, there exists the abstract entity triangularity, and besides the two lamp posts, there exists the number two. In Rule 14 of the *Regulae* Descartes denies the existence of abstract mathematical entities.[53] He holds that pure geometry, like physics, has for its subject matter concrete existence but differs from physics in two respects. First, the propositions of geometry are true, whether physical bodies exist or do not exist. This is obviously not the case in physics. Second, the student of geometry confines his study to bodies only insofar as they possess figure. The physicist, on the other hand, studies bodies also with respect to their possessing depth and being capable of motion. There are no abstract entities, says Descartes; there are only abstract studies of concrete objects: "... If we are dealing with figure, let us remember that we [as pure mathematicians] are concerned with an extended subject, though we restrict ourselves to conceiving it merely as possessing figure. When body is the object, let us reflect that we are dealing with the very same thing, taken as possessing length, breadth and depth."[54]

In physics, unlike mathematics, we do make categorical claims about existent things. Descartes, nevertheless, held that the sciences of nature cannot provide us with the first principle. Here again he differed from the Scholastics who had assumed that the first principle in the order of discovery was that material bodies exist. According to them, we must first be certain of physical existence before we can demonstrate the existence of God and that of the incorporeal soul. Descartes challenged this position for two reasons. First, the science of physics is ultimately based on the intuition of certain simple natures (figure, extension, and motion). No doubt the ideas of these simple natures are clear and distinct in the sense that I can know certain necessary truths about them. But these truths are hypothetical, like the propositions of pure geometry, for I can clearly conceive the nonexistence of material bodies. Second, prior to establishing certain metaphysical truths, I can entertain serious reasons for denying that my sensory experiences provide certainty in my belief that the physical world exists. Descartes' position is that prior to discovering the principles of metaphysics, the physical conception of the world is no less a hypothetical construction respecting existence than is Euclidean geometry.

But how are we going to discover this first principle? At any time in a man's life there are many propositions about existent things that he feels are certainly true. How is he going to discover that "being whose existence is known to us better than that of any other, so that it can serve as a principle to discover them." The discovery must be made from some original position in which for the first time he is going to inquire into what exists. He must on the one hand be a mature man with all his developed faculties and with a consciousness on how to proceed methodically; but, on the other hand, like a child, his mind for the first time starts on a journey of discovering what exists. Unlike the child who is guided by certain natural instincts, he will be guided by the pure understanding alone. But how is this original position, from which the journey to truth is going to commence, to be achieved? Descartes' answer is that one must find the means of liberating oneself from all prejudices. There is only one way for accomplishing this task, namely, by trying to adopt a skeptical attitude toward all of one's beliefs.

CHAPTER 3

Skepticism

DESCARTES' attempt to adopt a skeptical attitude toward all of his beliefs as a prelude to the discovery of the first principle is to be found in the *Meditations, Discourse,* the *Principles* and *The Search After Truth.* We shall, however, in the main, though not exclusively, concern ourselves with his presentation of it in the *Meditations* because in this work he presents his case in the most detailed and persuasive manner:

> It is now some years since I detected how many were the false beliefs that I had from the earliest youth admitted as true, and how doubtful was everything I had since constructed on this basis; and from that time I was convinced that I must once and for all seriously undertake to rid myself of all the opinions which I had formerly accepted, and commence to build anew from the foundation, if I wanted to establish any firm and permanent structure in the Sciences.[1]

In emphasizing the term "I" in the above passage, Descartes is referring to himself, but not to himself at the time of his writing the *Meditations.* Descartes began his *Meditations,* as Professor Harry Frankfurt rightfully claims, by adopting the point of view of an intellectually unsophisticated person who has not yet performed any philosophical and scientific inquiry and "who has always been guided more or less unreflectively in his opinions by common sense."[2] Descartes explicitly makes this point in his *Conversation with Burman,* wherein he states that in the *First Meditations* he is representing himself not as a man of science but as a novice who is first beginning to philosophize.[3]

It is apparent from the passage quoted above that Cartesian skepticism is a method adopted by the mind for the purpose of liberating itself from prejudices in order to discover the foundations (the first principle) of all the sciences. The passage is, however, incomplete in two respects. First, Descartes does not explain why it is not possible for a person to have firm and certain scientific beliefs without knowledge of the foundations. Second, he does not give us any illustrations of those beliefs which he had accepted as true from his earliest childhood and upon which all his other opinions are based. This situation can be remedied by consulting other texts. In his reply to the seventh set of objections Descartes says that, thanks to his skeptical venture, he is able to distinguish those beliefs which he can doubt from those which he cannot and, had he not performed this task, "the presence of the former should produce a general uncertainty about all."[4] Descartes is not denying that a person can discover scientific truths without knowledge of the foundations, but such a person can never be secure no matter how carefully he reasons and experiments from becoming a skeptic. Cartesian skepticism is the only insurance policy that a person can take out to secure himself from genuine skepticism. As for Descartes' failure to illustrate those beliefs which he had acquired in his early childhood, this oversight is remedied by a passage in the *Principles*:

And afterwards, when the machine of the body which has been so constituted by nature, that it can of its own inherent power turn here and there, by turning fortuitously this way and the other, followed after what was useful and avoided what was harmful, the mind which was closely allied to it, reflecting on the things which it followed after or avoided, remarked first of all that they existed outside itself, and attributed to them not alone magnitudes, figures, movements, and other such properties which it apprehended as things or modes of things, but also tastes and smells, and the like, the sensations of which it perceived that these things caused in it. And as all other things were only considered in so far as they served for the use of the body in which it was immersed, mind judged that there was more or less reality in each body, according as the impressions made on body were more or less strong. Hence came the belief that there was much more substance or corporeal reality in rocks or metals than in air or water, because the sensations of hardness and weight were much more strongly felt. And thus it was that air was only regarded as anything when it was agitated by some wind, and we experienced it to be either hot or cold.[5]

The foundations of the unreflective man's beliefs is the principle that reality is as it appears to the senses: that bodies are not only extended but possess color and smell as well; that rocks and metals have more substantial reality than air and water. Man, Descartes teaches us, is a body-mind complex and, prior to philosophizing, his beliefs are the result of his concern with the welfare and preservation of his body; and since nature, having, so to speak, programmed him to rely on his senses for this purpose, he accepts their deliverances at face value. True, it is the mind alone which perceives and judges, but the evidence upon which it relies for its judgments is derived from the senses and the imagination. It is not that the ordinary man never perceives the objects of the pure understanding; rather, because he cannot distinguish sensory from intellectual matters, he never perceives things clearly and distinctly. "There are even a number of people who throughout all their lives perceive nothing so correctly as to be capable of judging of it properly."[6] They are unable to distinguish the figures, lines, and points in their imagination from the pure mathematical concepts of figure, line, and point; consequently they judge erroneously that mathematical propositions and, for that matter, all necessary truths are grounded on sense experience. When Hobbes was puzzled as to why Descartes tried to adopt a skeptical attitude toward all his beliefs, Descartes' answer was that his purpose was to prepare the reader's mind "for the study of intellectual matters and for distinguishing them from matters corporeal, a purpose for which such [skeptical] arguments seem wholly necessary."[7]

In the *Regulae* Descartes held that a study of pure mathematics is a good intellectual training for developing a facility in applying the rules of method. We now see that Descartes believed that this training can also be accomplished by a provisional adoption of a skeptical attitude toward all of one's beliefs. There is, however, a crucial difference in the two cases. Training in mathematics cannot prepare the mind for the discovery of the first principles of knowledge (metaphysics) because, as indicated previously, while in the case of mathematics the senses and the understanding are in agreement, this is not so in metaphysics:

For, though in their own nature they [the primary notions of meta-physics] are as intelligible as, or even more intelligible than those the geometricians study, yet being contradicted by the many pre-conceptions of our senses to which we have since our earliest years been accustomed, they cannot be perfectly apprehended except by those who give studious attention and study to them, and withdraw their minds as far as possible from matters corporeal.[8]

This withdrawing of the mind from things corporeal, as a prelude to the discovery of metaphysical truth, is accomplished by Cartesian skepticism. This same sentiment is expressed by Descartes in the synopsis of the *First Meditation*: "In the *First Meditation* I set forth the reasons for which we may, generally speaking, doubt about all things and *especially about material things. . . .*"[9] A note of caution is here in order. Descartes is neither asserting nor implying that in all scientific activity we should discard our sense experiences but only that we should do so for the purpose of discovering the foundations of all the sciences, namely, the first principles of knowledge (metaphysics).

Methodological skepticism, like all intellectual activity, re-quires rules of procedure to guide the mind in its undertaking. The first rule has to do with the fact that a person has, except in his earliest childhood, an incredible number of beliefs in his mind and were he to try to induce a skeptical attitude toward each of them separately, he would die before he accomplished his task. According to the first rule, he has to sort out his beliefs into different categories, based on differences in the criteria which he has used from earliest childhood to judge propositions to be true or false. For instance, those beliefs grounded on sense perception belong to one category, those on authority to another. The reason for organizing beliefs in this manner is that if any criterion is found defective, all the beliefs grounded on it are no longer to be accepted as true. The second rule sets the criterion for distinguishing those beliefs which ought to be brought within "the sphere of the doubtful" from those which ought not. Why, for instance, ought a person to adopt a skeptical attitude toward the proposition "I am at present awake" and not toward "I feel pain"? Descartes' rule is that, if a person is able to think of some reason, not necessarily a sufficient one, for rejecting a proposition which he presently holds to be true, he should at once suspend accepting it as true and place it within "the sphere of the doubtful." It is the only way, says Descartes, that a person can protect himself from ever being convinced that something is true which is not certain and indubitable. In the *First Meditation* he writes:

Now for this object [methodological skepticism] it is not necessary that I should show that all of these are false—I shall perhaps never arrive at this end. But inasmuch as reason already persuades me that I ought no less carefully to withhold my assent from matters which are not entirely certain and indubitable than from those which appear to me manifestly to be false, if I am able to find in each one some reason to doubt, this will suffice to justify my rejecting the whole. And for that end it will not be requisite that I should examine each in particular, which would be an endless undertaking; for, owing to the fact that the destruction of the foundation of necessity brings with it the downfall of the rest of the edifice, I shall only in the first place attack those principles upon which all my former opinions rested.[10]

When the reader studies the *First Meditation*, he ought to keep in mind that the *First Meditation*, on a first, or even a second, reading, appears to consist in a series of skeptical arguments for an identical conclusion. This view, however, is misleading. There is a continuous dialectical development of Descartes' skeptical position as he realizes the limitations of each of his conclusions for his skeptical purpose until he arrives at the Demon hypothesis. With this fact in mind, the *First Meditation* can be divided into three parts. In the first part, Descartes argues for the conclusion that he has no reason to be certain that his senses provide him with reliable information about the physical world. He does not, however, at this stage of his argument, claim that we do not have an adequate basis for believing that there is a physical world. This first part ends with the famous dream argument. In the second part, Descartes probes the implications of the fact that he might possibly never have been awake; this phase terminates in his concluding that he has no reason to be absolutely certain that there exists a world of bodies. In the third part, Descartes introduces the hypothesis of a malignant demon for the purpose of changing his position from that of doubting that there is a world to the assumption that there is none on the ground that a very powerful demon is deceiving him.

Descartes does not consider the arguments he accepts in the *First Meditation* as good ones but as adequate at the initial stage of inquiry before he has discovered certain metaphysical truths. In the *Sixth Meditation*, after Descartes has discovered the indubitability of his own existence as a thinking being and that of God, he will then feel able to demonstrate the inadequacy of all his arguments in the *First Meditation*. Descartes makes this point in one of his replies to Hobbes. "I dealt with skeptical arguments in the *First Meditation*," he writes, "because I intended to reply to these very arguments in the subsequent meditations; and partly in order to show the strength of the truths I afterwards propound by the fact that such metaphysical doubts cannot shake them."[11]

I *The First Argument Against the Senses*

In presenting his first skeptical argument Descartes writes: "All that up to the present time I have accepted as most true and certain I have learned either from the senses or through the senses, but it is sometimes proved to me that these senses are deceptive, and it is wiser not to trust entirely to anything by which we have once been deceived."[12] The phrase "from the senses and through the senses" is used to make a distinction between those beliefs which are derived from personal sense experience and those based on hearsay. A belief, for instance, that a body has a certain color is "derived from the senses" if a person has seen the colored body. Whereas many opinions are accepted on the authority of teachers and parents, these are accepted "through the senses," namely, by hearing them made by those who are considered to be authoritative.

Descartes gives us no illustrations of the deceptiveness of the senses in the texts of the *First Meditation* but does so in the sixth wherein he restates the argument. He there gives an example of towers which from afar appear to be round but on closer inspection seem to be square and of the statues on top of these towers which, when viewed from the bottom of the towers, appear to be small but, when viewed from a different position, seem to be much larger. Descartes also speaks there of the deception of the internal as well as of the external senses. His example of the former is that of people whose arms and legs are amputated but yet seem to feel pain in their amputated parts. Descartes uses illusions as examples of the deceptiveness of his senses. This usage seems important in understanding what he intended to establish in his argument, for there is a difference between an illusion and an hallucination. A discussion of the sense of vision will illustrate this, though what is said of it applies to the other senses as well. In the case of an illusion, the person sees a body, but it looks to him in some respect to be other than it is. He actually sees a stick half immersed in water but it is straight, whereas visually it appears to be bent. On the other hand, when a person has an hallucination, we say that he sees nothing, though it appears to him that he is seeing something. In Shakespeare's play, Macbeth thought that he saw a dagger, but there was no dagger to be seen. Since Descartes' examples of sense deception are illusions, I believe that in this first argument Descartes did not intend to establish that we can never be certain of the existence of physical bodies but only that we can never be certain that the information about the physical world conveyed by our senses is reliable. Had Descartes intended to cast doubt on the very existence of the physical world, he would have to mean by "sense deception" nothing less than an hallucination.

I believe that Descartes' first argument is a poor one. As we shall shortly see, so does Descartes, but my reason for thinking it is a poor argument is different from that of Descartes! In order to develop my criticism, I shall have to make a distinction between an illusion and a delusion. A delusion can be defined as an error in judgment partly caused by an illusion or an hallucination. When I was a child, not only did tracks at a distance visually appear to converge, as they still do; but I was terrified because I was convinced that they actually converged. With the exception of early childhood rarely do the many illusions we experience delude us. We are not taken in by elliptical looking pennies, by ocean liners which, at a distance, look no larger than my hand, by sticks which appear to be bent in water, and so on. Keeping this distinction in mind, we can distinguish two different questions. The first is whether as the result of our sense experiences we can have certain knowledge about the physical world? And the second is whether, respecting any one of our sense experiences, we can be certain that it is not illusory. Descartes, I believe, took it for granted that an affirmative answer to the first depends on an affirmative answer to the second.

I do not think that it does. One has only to reflect on the fact that vision, which is the sense which provides us with the largest amount of information about the physical world also provides us with the greatest number of illusions. It seems conceivable that if all our sense experiences were illusory in one respect or another, we might yet be certain, and have reason to be certain, about many facts pertaining to the physical world. This is possible because the human mind, on the basis of its sense experiences, formulates a system of hypotheses as a result of which it can predict what its future experiences will be under certain conditions. It can also explain the sensory illusions on grounds of perspective, the function of the organs, or the distorting effects of the medium. What is essential for our having certainty in belief about the physical world is that we must initially accept a number of sense experiences as veridical and nonillusory. But, in accepting them for the purpose of coordinating them, we need not be certain of their veridical status. We need only declare that every sense experience is innocent until proven guilty.

It has been previously mentioned that Descartes rejected his first argument. Let us see what his reason was for doing so:

But it may be that although the senses sometimes deceive us concerning things which are hardly perceptible, or very far away, there are yet many others to be met with as to which we cannot reasonably have any doubt, although we recognize them by their means. For example, there is the fact that I am here, seated by the fire, attired in a dressing gown, having this paper in my hands and other similar matters.[13]

Descartes is distinguishing, which he had failed to do in the first argument, between those sense experiences which he has under ideal conditions from those which he had under improper ones. He can doubt their reliability in the latter case but not in the former. When an object is at a distance, or very small, or when the illumination is poor, he can doubt what he appears to see but not when the object is close at hand, large, and when seen under ideal conditions of illumination.

But then Descartes considers a possible reason for doubting his sense experiences even under ideal external conditions. He might possibly be a defective observer, even to the point of being insane:

And how could I deny that these hands and this body are mine, were it not perhaps that I compare myself to certain persons, devoid of sense, whose cerebella are so troubled and clouded by violent vapours of black bile, that they constantly assure us that they are kings when they are really quite poor, or that they are clothed in purple when they are really without covering, or who imagine that they have an earthenware head or are nothing but pumpkins or are made of glass. [Descartes, however, dismisses the above as a reason for doubting his sense experiences under ideal external conditions.] But they are mad and I should not be any the less insane were I to follow examples so extravagant.[14]

Descartes is convinced that he is not insane for two reasons. The first is that the insane have a certain brain condition, that is, they are those "whose cerebella" are troubled by "violent vapours of black bile," which is not true of himself. Second, the insane make wild and extravagent claims; he does not. These reasons presuppose that the people whom Descartes, together with the majority of human beings, labels as "insane" are in fact insane. How can Descartes be certain about this matter? Might it not be that those who are considered to be insane are really the privileged observers and that Descartes and the vast majority of mankind are mad? Despite this possibility, Descartes had to ignore this issue. As a person who is meditating and trying to engage his readers in this activity, he has to assume that he is a sane observer and thinker so that he can speak in the name of any rational being as does any philosopher and scientist who formulates an argument.

II   *The Dream Argument*

Having satisfied himself that the external conditions of perception are at present ideal and that he is a sane observer, Descartes proceeds to raise another objection which challenges his right to be convinced that he is seated by a fireplace in his nightgown:

At the same time I must remember that I am a man, and that consequently I am in the habit of sleeping, and in my dreams, representing to myself the same things or sometimes even less probable things, than do those who are insane in their waking moments. How often has it happened to me that in the night I dreamt that I found myself in this particular place, that I was dressed and seated near the fire, whilst in reality I was lying undressed in bed! At this moment it does indeed seem to me that it is with eyes awake that I am looking at this paper; that this head which I move is not asleep, that it is deliberately and of set purpose that I extend my hand and perceive it; what happens in sleep does not appear so clear nor so distinct as does all this. But in thinking over this I remind myself that on many occasions I have in sleep been deceived by similar illusions, and in dwelling carefully on this reflection *I see so manifestly that there are no certain indications by which we may clearly distinguish wakefulness from sleep* that I am lost in astonishment. And my astonishment is such that it is almost capable of persuading me that I now dream.[15]

This is an important argument and, with the exception of his *Cogito ergo sum* ("I think, therefore I am") and his distinction between body and mind, there is no reasoning employed by Descartes which has received so much critical commentary. But, before we consider a very small part of this commentary, we had better understand precisely what Descartes is saying.

Descartes begins the dream argument with the comment that he often dreamed that highly improbable things were taking place, the kinds of things that are even less likely to happen than what insane people believe to take place. Let us call such dreams "wild dreams." But what Descartes seems to be experiencing at present, namely, that he is seated by a fireplace in a nightgown, is not, however, an improbable situation; and so he cannot conclude on the basis of his experience that he is dreaming. But then he reminds himself that not all dreams are wild; in fact, he had in the past dreamed that he was in the exact same situation in which at present he takes himself to be in. He hesitates, however, to draw his skeptical conclusion, "What happens in dreams does not appear to be so clear nor so distinct as does all this." The term "clear" in this context means vivid; Descartes, like Hume, believed that the vividness of an experience contributed to a person's conviction that what he was experiencing was something real. And "distinct" means sufficiently vivid so that all the elements that make up the experience are clearly distinguishable. Descartes, however, cannot be certain on the basis of the above two criteria that he is awake, since dreams are occasionally "clear and distinct" in the above sense. Descartes then concludes that he cannot be certain that he is awake since there are no certain indications that would differentiate dreaming from waking.

Descartes' conclusion is open to two different interpretations: (1) at any time that I believe that I am awake I have no right to be certain that this belief is true; (2) I have no right to be certain that I am awake at present nor that I have ever been awake at any previous time. Clearly (1) does not entail (2); for it is conceivable that on every occasion when I believe that I am awake I do not know this to be true, yet I might know that I was awake at some time in the past. I might possibly even know which of my past experiences were waking states and which were not. On the other hand (2) entails (1). Obviously (2) is the stronger skeptical position and (1) the weaker one. Which of these two interpretations is Descartes'? I am inclined to believe that (2), the stronger thesis, was Descartes' conclusion. I base this on two considerations.

First, immediately after the dream argument Descartes writes: "Now let us assume that we are asleep and that all these particulars, e.g. that we open our eyes, shake our head, extend our hands, and so on, are but false delusions; and let us reflect that possibly neither our hands nor our whole body are such as they appear to us to be."[16] This passage suggests the likelihood that Descartes is uncertain that he has ever been awake, though he seems to remain convinced that he has a body. Second, in the *Search After Truth*, Descartes has Eudoxus, one of the characters in the dialogue, present a short version of the dream argument and then conclude: "How can you be certain that *your life is not a perpetual dream* and all that you imagine you learn by means of your senses is not as false now as it is when you sleep?"[17] Again, from the *Discourse*, we have the following, "And since all the same thoughts and conceptions which we have while awake may also come to us in sleep, without any of them being at that time true, I resolved to assume *that everything that ever entered into my mind was no more true than the illusions of my dreams*."[18] The fact that Descartes in both the *Search after Truth* and the *Discourse* adopted the stronger skeptical conclusion constitutes a *prima facie* case that he adopted the same conclusion for the dream argument in the *Meditations*.

There are, however, two reasons why one might be inclined to accept the weaker skeptical thesis as being Descartes' conclusion. First, Descartes, in the dream argument, distinguishes wild dreams from nonwild ones. Dreaming that a woman is turning into a salamander is an example of a wild dream, whereas dreaming that he is seated by a fire in his nightgown is not. But, in order to classify dreams in this manner, Descartes had to be able to identify a number of past experiences as waking states. How else could he have come to believe that there are certain laws of nature which his wild dreams appear to violate? The above consideration should not lead us to abandon the strong skeptical thesis. What Descartes required, in order to distinguish wild dreams from nonwild ones, is not knowledge, but, prior to the dream argument, acceptance without question, that some of his past experiences constituted waking states. The strong skeptical conclusion is perfectly consistent with Descartes' having employed a criterion by which he distinguished what he believed, but did not know, were waking states from dream states. As a result of this procedure, he came to believe that there are certain laws of nature, which he consequently employed to distinguish wild from nonwild dreams.

Second, immediately after the dream argument, and despite

the fact that Descartes is no longer convinced that he is presently awake, he continues to be certain that a physical world exists. But how could he have retained this conviction unless he was also convinced that at some time in the past he had been awake and perceived physical bodies? Again, we need not abandon the strong skeptical thesis by drawing this latter conclusion from the text. Descartes could have held the position that, despite the fact that he may never have been awake, his body, in some inexplicable fashion, supplied his imagination with raw material for the composition of his dreams. In point of fact, this condition occasionally does occur. For example, while one is asleep, a cold wind may chill one's body and cause one to dream that one is stranded in a snow drift. It is important to bear in mind what has been stated previously that, in the *First Meditation*, Descartes is representing a person who is philosophizing for the first time. When such a person first entertains the possibility that he may never have been awake, he does not immediately conceive himself to be a disembodied mind fabricating dreams, but rather a living human, which includes his body, sleeping throughout a lifetime with his body supplying his imagination with data for the construction of his dreams.

Considering the two matters discussed above, there appears to be no reason to abandon the position that Descartes' skeptical conclusion was the stronger thesis.

III *From the Dream Argument to the Demon*

Descartes is no longer certain that he is presently awake or, for that matter, that he has ever been awake; but this uncertainty does not undermine his conviction in the existence of the physical world. The problem he now confronts is, What can I know with certainty about the physical world? The answer to this question, he thinks, lies in considering what the powers and limits of the imagination are in constructing dream objects and events. This appears to be a sensible procedure once one accepts, as does Descartes at this stage in the *First Meditation*, that the data provided to the imagination for the construction of dreams represent real objects. But how is one going to go about discovering the powers and limits of the dreamer's imagination? Descartes had a ready answer to this question. One can make this discovery by drawing an analogy between the imagination of an artist in painting figures on canvas and the imagination of the dreamer in constructing dream objects. The imagination is, after all, the same in both cases.

Descartes first considers the artist who paints satyrs and nymphs. The artist paints these fictitious figures by putting together parts which represent the limbs of actual animals. In an identical fashion, the imagination of the dreamer composes dream objects out of parts like hands, arms, and legs, which represent real physical bodies. On the basis of this comparison, Descartes, while no longer certain that the complex figures in his dream represent physical bodies, remains convinced that their parts do: "For, as a matter of fact, painters, even when they study with the greatest skill to represent sirens and satyrs by forms the most strange and extraordinary, cannot give them natures which are entirely new, but merely make a certain medley of the members of different animals . . ."[19] But Descartes immediately realizes that he has underestimated the ingenuity and creative skill of both the imagination of the artist and that of the dreamer. A truly creative artist can create not only a fictitious complex figure but compose it out of purely fictitious parts so that nothing even remotely like it has ever been seen. This creative ingenuity is true of the imagination of the dreamer as well. A dream object need not resemble either as a whole or in its parts a physical body. There is, however, a limit to the power and skill of the imagination of both artist and dreamer. While the painted figure may be totally fictitious, the elements out of which it is composed, for instance its colors, cannot be fabricated by the imagination and consequently are not fictitious.

Analogously, the dreamer's imagination does not have the ability to originate the basic elements with which it works. There are certain "simple and universal things" out of which our dreams are composed by the imagination which are "real and true." These "simple and universal" elements turn out to be the simple natures of the *Regulae* which are either purely material or else common to mind and matter. Descartes writes: "To such a class of things pertains corporeal nature in general, and its extension, the figure of extended things, their quantity or magnitude and number, as also the place in which they are, the time which measures their duration, and so on."[20] There is, however, a crucial difference between the introduction of the simples in the *Regulae* and in the *First Meditation*. In the former work they are the objects of intellectual intuition, whereas in the *First Meditation* Descartes discovers them by inspecting what he considers might possibly be dream objects and events. This difference is not a minor matter; for in intuiting the clear and distinct ideas of simple natures, the mind is able to trace the necessary connections by which they are related to each other; whereas no necessary connections are revealed as a result of inspecting the objects of the senses or the imagination. For Descartes, in the *First Meditation*, the fact that these simple natures are found together and are the ultimate elements of physical existence is a contingent truth which might have been otherwise.

The only certainty Descartes has about physical bodies is that, like dream objects, they are composed of simple elements such as extension, figure, and so on. All his former beliefs about composite bodies such as his hands and feet, the earth, and the moon might possibly be false, for he may never have been awake and his imagination may have composed objects which do not even remotely resemble material bodies. This contrast, between the simple natures whose existence he cannot doubt and the composite bodies whose existence he can, leads Descartes to draw a distinction between the sciences. Physics, astronomy, and medicine deal with composite bodies; consequently the propositions accepted in these sciences are to be considered dubious and uncertain. On the other hand, the propositions of arithmetic and geometry which have as their subject matter those "very simple and very general" natures are to be considered as having "some measure of certainty. . . . For whether I am awake or asleep two and three together always form five . . ."[21]

Descartes at this stage in the *First Meditation* is certain of only two things: there exists a physical world which consists of simple natures, such as extension, figure, quantity, and so on, and the simple propositions of arithmetic and geometry. These two certainties are related; for Descartes, at this stage of the

Meditations, does not as yet think of the mathematical sciences as purely abstract and hypothetical but believes that mathematical propositions are categorical statements about the physical simples. Descartes now proceeds to challenge the above two certainties. He first considers the possibility that there is no physical universe:

> Nevertheless I have long had fixed in my mind the belief that an all-powerful God existed by whom I have been created such as I am. But how do I know that He has not brought it to pass that there is no earth, no heaven, no extended body, no magnitude, no place, and that nevertheless [I possess the perceptions of all these things and that] they seem to me to exist just exactly as I now see them?[22]

After the dream argument, Descartes continued to assume that a physical world existed, for how else could the imagination have procured the data for its activity in constructing dream objects and events. Having granted to the imagination the greatest ingenuity that this faculty is capable of, he concluded that "certain simple and general" natures constitute the raw material upon which it operates. Consequently, he felt certain that there exists one or more bodies which are extended, possess figure, magnitude, and so on. But now he entertains the possibility that it is not his body which supplies his imagination with the simples but a very different agency, namely, God. God, however, can, if he is sufficiently powerful and ingenious, supply the imagination with data for the construction of dreams without there existing anything external to God's thought or his own imagination which conforms to the data. In other words, there may possibly be no physical world, but it may be that God supplies the imagination with the ideas of the physical simples for its construction of a seeming world.

Two facts are worth taking notice of regarding the above. It is obvious to Descartes that the imagination cannot totally fabricate dreams, that it has to receive the raw material for its task from some external agent. He first thinks of this external agent as his own body and subsequently as God. But at no point in the *First Meditation* does he consider his own mind as the possible agent, for he has as yet not developed a concept of mind as a result of which he could entertain this as a possibility. He does not articulate such a concept until the *Second Meditation*. Second, in the *First Meditation* Descartes does not consider the implications pertaining to the nature of his own existence in the fact that there may perhaps be no physical world. Again this matter is not considered until the *Second Meditation*. Both of the above points bring out a significant fact about the *First Meditation*. In this meditation Descartes' mind is operating with concepts which he had acquired from early childhood and which originated primarily from the senses and the imagination. Now, so long as he has not revised at least one of these concepts (Descartes will revise the concept of himself in the *Second Meditation*), he will continue to be a person who can think of no other source of knowledge than that of the senses. True, he now suspects that this source may not provide him with knowledge. But he has as yet not discovered the pure understanding as a distinct faculty from that of the senses and the imagination. Notice that when Descartes in the *First Meditation* uses terms like "certainty" and "indubitability," he qualifies them. He speaks of "some measure of certainty" and of "an element of indubitability." Why so? Because, not having distinguished the senses from the pure understanding, he does not, in the *First Meditation*, clearly and distinctly perceive any proposition, including mathematical propositions, to be true.

The certainty and indubitability in the *First Meditation* is that of an intellectually unsophisticated person who accepts certain matters without question. This conclusion is borne out by the fact that Descartes in the *First Meditation* is able to be certain about some matter at one stage and then become uncertain about it at some subsequent stage. If he were certain as a result of a clear and distinct perception, then he could not subsequently doubt the same matter. What I have just stated is borne out by Descartes' skepticism regarding simple mathematical propositions which appears in the *First Meditation*: "And, besides, as I sometimes imagine that others deceive themselves in the things which they think they know best, how do I know that I am not deceived every time that I add two and three, or count the sides of a square, or judge of things yet simpler, if anything simpler can be imagined?"[23]

One of Descartes' central doctrines is that a person cannot, when he has a clear and distinct perception of a proposition, doubt its truth. It would have been impossible for Descartes to have escaped from skepticism had he not persistently maintained this position. But we see that he is uncertain of the truth of the simplest mathematical propositions. The most likely conclusion is that Descartes, in the *First Meditation*, was not taking himself to be perceiving mathematical propositions clearly and distinctly, but rather in a confused way—"never in the abstract and separated from matter and from particular instances." Granting that Descartes does not perceive that two and three make five or that a square has four sides clearly and distinctly; nevertheless he had, in my opinion, no grounds for no longer feeling certain of their truth for the reason he gave above. No doubt people feel certain about the truth of many propositions which are false. And many people in Descartes' time were as certain that the earth is a stationary body as they were that two and three make five. But why should the falsehood of the former lead one to doubt that possibly the latter is false as well? The evidence for the one may be very different from the evidence of the other. What Descartes had to show for the purpose of generating doubt that "two and three make five" is that even when people carefully and diligently consider *simple* mathematical propositions, they occasionally fall into error.

At this point in the *First Meditation* Descartes has reached the goal of his initial inquiry, which was to consider whether he could bring all the beliefs which he was formerly certain about "within the sphere of the doubtful." The answer is that he could. Bear in mind that all the things he was formerly certain about he had learned, as he says in the beginning of the *First Meditation*, "either from the senses or through the senses." After the dream argument, Descartes had remained certain about the existence of the simple physical natures and the truths of the propositions about them which constituted the sciences of arithmetic and geometry. But now that these certainties have been abandoned, there are no propositions which he had formerly believed which are not for him now dubious and uncertain.

But then, what of Descartes' own existence and the "common notions" which, in the *Principles*, he called "eternal truths," such as "it is impossible that the same thing should be and should not be?" In the *First Meditation*, Descartes does not consider the issue of his own existence. Nevertheless, since he has as yet no conception of himself as distinct from his body, in doubting the existence of the physical world, he is indirectly doubting his own existence. I am not suggesting that, if in the *First Meditation* Descartes had entertained the proposition "I exist," he could have doubted it. What I claim is that, given his confused conception of himself, in doubting that "there exists physical bodies," he doubts the truth of a proposition which, if it were false, would entail his nonexistence insofar as he exemplified the confused concept. As for the eternal truths, they have the same status as do mathematical propositions in the *First Meditation*. They are not abstracted "from matter and particular instances"; consequently, if the physical world does not exist, then the eternal truths are false. What Descartes, at this point in his meditation, takes himself to have demonstrated is that none of the beliefs which he had derived "from and through the senses" can serve as the foundation of the sciences. They are all exposed to skeptical doubt.

IV   *The Demon*

One would have expected Descartes to have ended the *First Meditation* once he achieved universal skepticism. But he did not. There were two things that concerned him. The first was his uneasiness about his having introduced God into his skeptical argument, and the second was the difficulty in maintaining the skeptical position after it was achieved.

Descartes, in the *First Meditation*, does not have a clear and distinct idea of God. Consequently, he cannot clearly perceive that an all-powerful being must be supremely good. He does, however, being a Christian, believe, on the basis of his faith, that these two properties belong to God. This latter fact presents him with a problem. How could God be supremely good and yet deceive him? Descartes' first thought on the matter was that He would not: "But possibly God has not desired that I should be thus deceived, for He is said to be supremely good."[24] But then Descartes reflects on the obvious fact that he is at least sometimes deceived, and he concludes from this that it may not be contrary to God's supreme goodness that he is always deceived: "If, however, it is contrary to His goodness to have made me such that I constantly deceive myself, it would also appear to be contrary to His goodness to permit me to be sometimes deceived, and nevertheless I cannot doubt that He does permit this."[25]

The idea of God as supremely good but possibly a deceiver is contrary to what Descartes is going to teach subsequently in the *Meditations*. One suspects that Descartes intended to show that we cannot rely merely on our faith in God's existence, when our conception of God is not clear and distinct, to liberate us from skepticism. We are not justified in saying: "Since a supremely good God exists [I accept this on faith], He would not permit me to believe that there is a physical world when in fact there is none." The obvious response to such reasoning is, "But then why does he allow you sometimes to fall into error." The intellectually unsophisticated believer is not able to meet this challenge because he has no clear and distinct idea of his own nature or of God's. He is not able to demonstrate that the fact that he sometimes falls into error is not incompatible with God's not being a deceiver. He has only two available positions: either goodness is incompatible with deception, hence God does not exist; or God exists, hence goodness is compatible with deception. In either case, he cannot use his faith in God's existence to save him from skepticism.

Descartes then tries to show that the atheist is in no better position than the believer with respect to avoiding skepticism. To demonstrate his point, Descartes makes two claims: the first is that to be in error is a defect, and the second is that the less exalted and powerful the source of a person's existence, the greater likelihood that the person is defective. From these two contentions he draws the conclusion that the less powerful the source of a person's existence, the more likely he is to err. But now the atheist attributes the source of a person's existence either "to fate or to accident, or make out that it is by a continual succession of antecedents, or by some other method . . ."[26]

Whichever one of these sources for human existence the atheist chooses, the source is less exalted and powerful than God. Consequently, it is more likely that universal deception is true of human beings if God does not exist than if He does.

The other matter which concerned Descartes after having arrived at the stage of total skepticism was the difficulty in maintaining it, for he noticed a tendency in himself to revert to the common sense beliefs which he had acquired from early childhood. He had difficulty, so to speak, keeping the lid on such former beliefs as his possessing hands and feet and the existence of the sun and the moon. There are two reasons for his difficulty. The mere fact that he was certain of the truth of these beliefs for many years gives them, he declares, a privileged position in his thinking: "For these ancient and commonly held opinions still revert frequently to my mind, long and familiar custom having given them the right to occupy my mind against my inclination and rendered them almost masters of my belief . . ."[27] Second, while he is no longer certain of their truth, nevertheless they are highly probable so that he has more reason for believing them to be true than for rejecting them. This tendency to revert to his former beliefs presents Descartes with a difficult problem; for, if he is going to discover the first principle of knowledge, he has to come up with some strategy for the purpose of maintaining his mind free from prejudices. He does, as the following passage indicates:

That is why I consider that I shall not be acting amiss, if, taking of set purpose a contrary belief, I allow myself to be deceived, and for a certain time pretend that all these opinions are entirely false and imaginary, until at last, having thus balanced my former prejudices with my latter [so that they cannot divert my opinions more to one side than to the other], my judgement will no longer be dominated by bad usage or turned away from the right knowledge of the truth.[28]

Before he had adopted this strategy, Descartes (to use an example) had suspended judging the proposition "there exists a sun" with respect to its truth or falsehood. One might say that he had adopted an agnostic position toward a belief in the existence of the sun. Unfortunately, he discovered that, against his will, he had a tendency to revert to his earlier belief. His new strategy is not to employ his will in order to suspend judgment respecting the existence of the sun but rather to direct it toward accepting the sun's nonexistence. In this way, his will, opting for the nonexistence of the sun, and his natural tendency to accept the sun's existence, will cancel each other; consequently his mind will be free from either prejudice. But how does one go about directing the will to judge improbable propositions to be true as the new strategy dictates? Descartes' answer to this question was to introduce the demon hypothesis:

I shall then suppose, not that God who is supremely good and the fountain of truth, but some evil genius not less powerful than deceitful, has employed his whole energies in deceiving me; I shall consider that the heavens, the earth, colours, figures, sound, and all other external things are naught but the illusions and dreams of which this genius has availed himself in order to lay traps for my credulity; I shall consider myself as having no hands, no eyes, no flesh, no blood, nor any senses, yet falsely believing myself to possess all these things; I shall remain obstinately attached to this idea, and if by this means it is not in my power to arrive at the knowledge of any truth, I may at least do what is in my power [that is, suspend my judgment], and with firm purpose avoid giving credence to any false thing, or being imposed upon by this arch deceiver, however powerful and deceptive he may be.[29]

CHAPTER 4

The Self

S HORTLY after reaching the stage of total skepticism, Descartes discovered that he could not doubt that he thinks and that consequently he must exist. This is the famous *Cogito, ergo sum* argument. Before the argument is examined, the significance of the context in which Descartes presented it is worth mentioning.

Cogito (let us, for brevity's sake, name the whole proposition *Cogito*), when stated in most contexts, is meaningless. Suppose you were strolling with your friend and, after conversing with him for a while, he says: "I think, therefore I am." Your friend's *Cogito* is contextually meaningless, in the sense that if he intended to use the expression to make an assertion, then he failed to do so because the context in which he uttered the statement precluded his succeeding. It is like two men strolling in the desert and one says to the other, "Close the door." The expression, given the desert surroundings, could not possibly express a command. No doubt one could *mention* the *Cogito* meaningfully in a lecture on Descartes, or use the propositional expression to shock, bewilder, or display a bit of stale humor, but what one could not do with it is to convey information. As "close the door," when uttered in a barren desert, cannot be obeyed or disobeyed, so the *Cogito* cannot inform or misinform. There is, however, one kind of nonphilosophical context which is an exception to the above claim. Imagine, in an automobile accident, a man flying out of his car and immediately after landing on the ground, saying, "Do I exist or do I not exist"; and then with a sigh of relief exclaiming, "But of course I exist, I am thinking."

Descartes' total skepticism about his former convictions, as outlined at the end of the previous chapter, provides a context in which the *Cogito* can be meaningfully asserted. Descartes was looking, as he says, for "Archimedes' point":

> Archimedes, in order that he might draw the terrestrial globe out of its place, and transport it elsewhere, demanded only that one point should be fixed and immovable; in the same way I shall have the right to conceive high hopes if I am happy enough to discover the one thing only which is certain and indubitable![1]

Archimedes' point, that is, the one proposition Descartes hopes to discover "which is certain and indubitable," will turn out to be the *Cogito*.

There is, however, a crucial difference between Descartes' *Cogito* and that of the man in the accident referred to above or, for that matter, to a person in any context other than total skepticism. The man in the accident perceives the *Cogito* clearly but cannot do so distinctly, whereas, in the *Second Meditation*, Descartes is in the position to perceive it both clearly and distinctly. The perception of the man in the accident is clear in that he cannot doubt that he exists once he has raised the issue. It is not, however, distinct since the "I," namely, himself, whose existence he cannot doubt, includes his body; and in including it, he is going beyond what is strictly warranted by the indubitable fact that he thinks. He could not possibly have avoided doing so, since he takes the reliability of his senses for granted and consequently has not the slightest doubt in the existence of bodies. On the other hand, Descartes, in the *Second Meditation*, precisely because of his skepticism, as we shall see below, was able to stay strictly within the confines of what is warranted by the evidence provided by the fact that he thinks. He was able to articulate a clear and distinct conception of himself, whose existence is indubitable, and which can serve as the first principle that lies at the foundation of all his scientific knowledge.

The *Cogito* argument is formulated in many places in Descartes' writings, including his replies to objections. The two most famous are to be found in the *Discourse* and in the *Meditations*. In the *Discourse* he writes:

But immediately afterwards I noticed that whilst I thus wished to think all things false, it was absolutely essential that the "I" who thought this should be somewhat, and remarking that this truth *"I think, therefore I am"* was so certain and so assured that all the most extravagent suppositions brought forward by the skeptics were incapable of shaking it, I came to the conclusion that I could receive it without scruple as the first principle of the Philosophy for which I was seeking.[2]

In the *Meditations*, the text reads as follows:

I myself, am I not at least something? But I have already denied that I had senses and body. Yet I hesitate, for what follows from that? Am I so dependent on body and senses that I cannot exist without these? But I was persuaded that there was nothing in all the world, that there was no heaven, no earth, that there were no minds, nor any bodies: was I not then likewise persuaded that I did not exist? Not at all; of a surety *I myself did exist since I persuaded myself of something* [or merely because I thought of something]. But there is some deceiver or other, very powerful and very cunning, whoever employs his ingenuity in deceiving me. Then without doubt, I exist also if he deceives me, and let him deceive me as much as he will, he can never cause me to be nothing so long as I think that I am something. So that after having reflected well and carefully examined all things, we must come to the definite conclusion that this proposition: I am, I exist, is necessarily true each time that I pronounce it, or that I mentally conceive it.[3]

There are clear differences in the two texts. *"Cogito, ergo sum"* appears in the *Discourse* but not in the *Meditations*. The closest to this latter proposition in the *Meditations* is the italicized sentence: "I myself did exist since I persuaded myself of something." Again, in the *Meditations*, Descartes refers to a demon who cannot deceive him respecting his conviction that he exists, but he makes no mention of this demon in the *Discourse*.

Despite these differences Descartes considered the two versions, and the many more that are scattered throughout his writings, as different formulations of the same argument. The important thing to bear in mind is Descartes' broad use of the word "thought": "What is a thing which thinks? It is a thing which doubts, understands [conceives], affirms, denies, wills, refuses, which also imagines and feels."[4] Consequently, instead of only using the verb "think" as the antecedent of "I am" (*sum*), Descartes can employ other verbs, as he sometimes does, such as "I doubt," "I persuaded myself," "I seem to see," and so on, as different forms of the same argument.

What kind of argument is *Cogito, ergo sum?* Is it a syllogism with an unstated universal premise? In that case, the argument would have the following form: Whatever thinks exists; I think; therefore I exist. No, says Descartes: "He who says '*I think hence I am, or exist*' does not deduce existence from thought by a syllogism, but, by a simple act of mental vision, recognizes it as if it were a thing that is known *per se*." I "see" in my own case that my thinking necessarily involves my existence and then and only then do I discover the indubitability of the proposition that everything that thinks exists. Descartes concludes, "For our mind is so constituted by nature that general propositions are formed out of the knowledge of particulars."[5] We must be careful not to misunderstand Descartes in this matter. He is not denying the obvious fact that the inference from *Cogito* ("I think") to *sum* ("I am") is deductively valid only if "whatever thinks exists" is included as a premise. But as he never fails to emphasize in all his writings, discovery of indubitable truth does not proceed in accordance with formal reasoning. In drawing *sum* from *Cogito*, I need never have thought of the general proposition that is formally required for the validity of the inference. True, when I infer *sum* ("I am") from *Cogito* ("I think") I display my knowledge that "whatever thinks exists"; for, unless I knew this general proposition to be true, I could not possibly have intuited the necessary connection between *Cogito* and *sum*; but this knowledge can only be said to be implicit in my mind, since I had never thought of the general proposition. It is implicit in the same sense as a person is said to have implicit knowledge of the rules of English syntax, because while he has never once thought of these rules, he nevertheless employs them in speaking English grammatically.

Granted that the argument is not a syllogism, does it nevertheless contain an inference? It definitely appears to, for in all of Descartes' formulations of the *Cogito* argument he employs the term *"ergo"* ("therefore" or "hence") which in ordinary usage signifies the presence of an inference. A good clue for understanding how Descartes regarded the *Cogito* argument lies in his response to one of Gassendi's criticisms. Gassendi was puzzled why Descartes confined his inference from thinking to existence. Why not "I walk, therefore I exist," or "I sing, therefore I exist." Such inferences are as legitimate as "I think, therefore I exist," declared Gassendi. Descartes' answer is instructive:

> When you say that *I could have inferred the same conclusion from any of my other actions*, you wander far from the truth, because there is none of my activities of which I am wholly certain . . . save thinking alone. For example you have no right to make the inference: "*I walk, hence I exist*," except insofar as our awareness of walking is a thought; it is of this alone that the inference holds good, not of the motion of the body, which sometimes does not exist, as in dreams, when nevertheless I appear to walk.[6]

Descartes is not contending that the inference from "I walk" to "I exist" is any less legitimate than from "I think" to "I exist." The nature of the inference is the same in both cases; there is an inference from the existence of a property (using the word "property" to designate states, acts, relations, as well as qualities) to the existence of the individual possessing the property. Where the two arguments differ is that the premise "I think" is indubitable, whereas "I walk" is not. I could believe that I am walking when in fact I am only dreaming that I am; but whether I am walking or not I cannot doubt that I think that I am walking. There are then, according to Descartes, two distinct intuitions involved in the *Cogito* argument: there is the intuition that "I think that I am walking" and the intuition that "I could not be having this thought unless I exist." The reason "I walk, hence I exist" will not serve Descartes' purpose in the *Second Meditation* is that in this case only one intuition is involved, namely "I could not be walking unless I exist." But, since I cannot be absolutely certain that I am walking I cannot have indubitable knowledge that I exist. Since there are two intuitions involved in the *Cogito* argument, its form is as follows: I think. Since I think, I exist.

The structure of the *Cogito* argument would seem to indicate that, unless a person inferred his existence from some fact about his thinking, he could reasonably doubt that he exists. Mystics and idealists have, after all, on some occasion in their lifetime denied their individual existence. But, and this is the thrust of Descartes' *Cogito* argument, a mystic could not reasonably deny his existence, no matter what the nature of his mystical experience was, if he kept before his mind the fact that he thought that he did not exist as distinct from being concerned with whether what he thought was true. The strength of *sum* as an indubitable proposition is that it is always available. No matter what is in a person's mind, he can always infer the indubitability of his own existence: "I am, I exist, is necessarily true each time that I pronounce it, or that I mentally conceive it." And if he is in a skeptical or mystical mood and says "I do not exist," he has merely to reflect on the fact that he entertains this proposition in his mind and he will immediately infer that it is false.

Why did Descartes believe that *sum*, in order to be known with absolute certainty, must be inferred from *Cogito*? The answer is to be found in the *Principles*:

But yet substance cannot be first discovered merely from the fact that it is a thing that exists, for that fact alone is not observed by us. We may, however, easily discover it by means of any one of its attributes because it is a common notion that nothing is possessed of no attributes, properties, or qualities. For this reason, when we perceive any attribute, we therefore conclude that some existing thing or substance to which it may be attributed, is necessarily present.[7]

Descartes is speaking about substance in general, physical as well as mental, but it applies also to a person's discovery of the indubitable fact that he exists. Descartes would agree with Hume who claimed, in the *Treatise*, that introspection never reveals the self. "For my part, when I enter most intimately into what I call *myself*, I always stumble on some particular perception or other, of heat or cold, light or shade, love or hatred, pain or pleasure."[8]

Descartes and David Hume, however, drew different conclusions from this alleged fact. Hume concluded that the self—

or mind—is not a substance but rather "a kind of theatre where several perceptions successively make their appearance."[9] Descartes, on the other hand, concluded that certain knowledge of the self's existence can only be obtained as the result of an inference from a mode or attribute of the self, that is, from what Hume called "a perception" and Descartes "a thought" (using this latter term in a very broad sense as indicated previously).

The above discussion provides a clue as to what has always puzzled Cartesian scholars. Is the term "I" in "I think" the same as, or different from, the "I" in "I exist"? If the meaning is the same, then Descartes' inference from *cogito* to *sum* is trivial in the same sense as the inference "This is a cow" from "this is a black cow"? How, then, could Descartes claim that *sum* is discovered from *cogito*? On the other hand, if the "I" differs in meaning in both cases, then the inference from *Cogito* to *sum* is illegitimate. Now it appears, from the above discussion that Descartes' position is that the "I" in "I think" is different from the "I" in "I exist." In the former case, "I" is a purely nominal subject and not a real one and is introduced only because there is no way of grammatically using a verb or an adjective without a subject. The "I" in "I exist" refers, however, to a real subject, that is, a substance. The inference, while formally invalid, is perfectly good on the ground that "no qualities or properties pertain to nothing; and that where some are perceived there must necessarily be some thing or substance on which they depend." What has to be added, from what has been said previously, is that the general proposition need never have been thought of by the person who intuits the necessary connection between "I think" and "I exist."

I *The Significance of the* Cogito *in Descartes' Philosophy*

A not uncommon position is that Descartes considered *Cogito, ergo sum* to have a privileged epistemological status in the sense that it is the most certain of all propositions including such eternal truths as "It is impossible that anything can be formed of nothing"; "That what has been done cannot be undone"; and so on. Thus Professor A. B. Gibson writes: ". . . they [the eternal truths] have to be affirmed objectively before they can be taken as true. Whereas, in the intuition of the self, subject and object are identical, so that there is no call for the reference, in all other cases so prejudicial to a world beyond."[10] And Professor S. V. Keeling expresses a similar attitude: "The difference lies in this: the *Cogito* disclosure provides *its own* evidence of clearness and distinctness, but the others do not."[11] The text of the *Meditations* and Descartes' replies to objections does not, on the face of it at any rate, bear out the special epistemological status given to it by these commentators. For instance, in one of his replies to the second set of objections Descartes writes:

But of those there are some so evident and at the same time so simple, that in their case we never doubt about believing them true: e.g., that I, while I think, exist; that what is once done cannot be undone, and other similar truths, about which clearly we can possess this certainty. For we cannot doubt them unless we think of them; but we cannot think of them without at the same time believing them to be true . . .[12]

Notice that *Cogito, ergo sum* is included with other "simple" and "evident" truths without the slightest hint that the former has a special status. It would appear that Descartes held all these propositions to be on the same epistemological level. A person is unable to doubt any one of these propositions once he entertains it in his mind.

Nor does Descartes anywhere assert or imply that, if a demon were deceiving him, he could reasonably doubt all propositions except *Cogito, ergo sum*. In fact, he seems explicitly to deny it: "Let who will deceive me, He can never cause me to be nothing while I think that I am, or some day cause it to be true to say that I have never been, it being true now to say that I am, or that two and three make more or less than five, or any such thing in which I see a manifest contradiction."[13]

What, then, is the significance of *Cogito, ergo sum*? There are, it would seem, any number of indubitable beliefs which might have constituted a challenge to total skepticism. Why did Descartes employ "I think, therefore I am" instead of, for instance, "whatever is once done cannot be undone"? There are, I believe, two reasons for his choice.

First, Descartes' methodological skepticism is initiated by a person who is philosophically unsophisticated. This person has as yet not differentiated the empirical application of mathematical propositions and other eternal truths from the *a priori* basis of their truth. He confuses the eternal truths with their concrete illustrations and is consequently in no position to perceive them clearly and distinctly. Thus, when he, so to speak, pretends that there is no world because a demon is causing him to have hallucinatory perceptions that there is one, he regards the eternal truths as false. When Descartes says, in his reply to the second set of objections, as quoted above, that a person cannot entertain certain propositions in his mind and at the same time doubt their truth, he is thinking of those propositions as clearly and distinctly perceived. And when, in the *Third Meditation*, he says, as quoted above, that a demon cannot deceive him regarding those matters whose denial would constitute "a manifest contradiction," he is again thinking of a person who perceives these matters clearly and distinctly.

At what point, then, does our unsophisticated intellectual pilgrim reach the stage of enlightenment when he is able to distinguish sensory from intellectual matters and can therefore begin to perceive propositions clearly and distinctly? This achievement, I believe, occurs *immediately after* he discovers his own existence to be indubitable. It takes place as a result of his clarifying a conception of himself which is clear and distinct. It seems, then, that Professors Gibson and Keeling are correct in claiming that *Cogito, ergo sum* is epistemologically privileged. It is not, however, privileged in that, as clearly and distinctly perceived, it is more certain than the eternal truths. The privileged status of the *Cogito* is such that, unlike the eternal truths, a person cannot reasonably doubt its truth, irrespective as to whether he perceives the proposition clearly and distinctly. It is the one proposition which is available at all times against *total* skepticism by any human being, regardless of his level of intellectual sophistication.

Second, *Cogito, ergo sum* is an existential proposition in the sense that it makes a claim about existence. Not so the eternal truths for, when perceived clearly and distinctly, they are hypothetical propositions which are true whether there is a world or not. For instance, the proposition "if something comes into existence, then it must have a cause," is true whether anything came into existence, or even whether there exists anything at all. What Descartes sought in the *Meditations*, as he says at the very outset of his work, is the existential foundations for the construction of a scientific view of the world to replace his old confused one. Consequently, what Descartes requires for his first principle is an existential proposition; that is why the use of an eternal truth to challenge total skepticism—even if that truth were clearly and distinctly perceived—would not have served Descartes' overall purpose in the *Meditations*.

II Sum res cogitans

After establishing the indubitable fact that he exists, Descartes proceeds to argue that the only thing he can be certain about himself, keeping in mind that an all-powerful demon is deceiving him, is that "I am a being who thinks" (*Sum res cogitans*). This section is one of the most brilliant pieces of reasoning to be found in the *Meditations*, and we would do well to follow it carefully step by step. It begins with Descartes' question, What is this "I" whose existence I cannot doubt?

But I do not yet know clearly enough what I am, I who am certain that I am: and hence I must be careful to see that I do not imprudently take some other object in place of myself, and thus that I do not go astray in respect of this knowledge that I hold to be the most certain and most evident of all that I have formerly learned.[14]

Descartes is trying to clarify the *Cogito* argument. In that argument he identified himself by a certain description, for instance, as "he who doubts the existence of a physical world" and then inferred that he exists as the one who satisfied that description. But he has yet to explain why the *Cogito* argument demonstrates the certainty of *sum* under certain descriptions and fails to do so under others? Why, for instance, does "I think

that I am breathing" demonstrate the certainty of *sum* but not
"I am breathing"? To answer this question, there is a need
for clarifying the concept of the bearer of the term "I" in the
Cogito argument. This concept is already in Descartes' mind;
it is implicit in his understanding in the same sense in which
a triangle is implicit in a person's understanding before he
proceeds to discover its properties. The concept was formed in
Descartes' mind once he introduced the hypothesis of a deceiving
demon and discovered that despite the demon's machinations
he could not doubt his own existence. Descartes is concerned
that, unless he explicates this concept of himself, and becomes
aware of what it contains and what it does not, he is likely to
confuse it with some other conception of himself, a conception
that is not strictly warranted by the *Cogito* argument.

But how is Descartes going to proceed in this matter? Obviously, he had a conception of himself prior to the *Cogito*
argument. Why not examine this concept in order to discover
what there is regarding what he formerly believed himself to
be which he can doubt, and what he cannot, now that a demon
is deceiving him? In this way, he will explicate the concept
of himself that is strictly warranted by the *Cogito* argument.
He writes:

What then did I formerly believe myself to be? Undoubtedly I
believed myself to be a man. But what is a man? Shall I say a
reasonable animal? Certainly not; for then I should have to inquire
what an animal is, and what is reasonable; and thus, from a single
question I should insensibly fall into an infinitude of others more
difficult; and I should not wish to waste the little time and leisure
remaining to me in trying to unravel subtleties like these.[15]

Descartes is not denying that he is a man. He merely feels
that such an answer is worthless at this stage of inquiry. The
concept of man is complex and the attempt to define it in the
manner of Scholastic philosophy will not render it intelligible.
The trouble with the Scholastic philosopher in this matter is
that he takes obscure ideas and arranges them by means of
definitions into genus and species. The genus, for instance, which
Descartes belongs to is animal and his species is man. As a

result of this procedure, one ends up with a neat and orderly classified system but without any clear and distinct ideas of the subject matter that is classified. Instead, Descartes seeks to discover those simple natures which he spoke about in the *Regulae*, which compose the self. When discovered, they should not be defined. "Further I declare that there are certain things which we render more obscure by trying to define them, because, since they are very simple and clear, we cannot know and perceive them better than by themselves."[16] Descartes is here, in the *Meditations*, as he had stated in one of his replies to the second set of objections, following the method of analysis which he had outlined in the *Regulae*.[17] He is trying to reduce complex phenomena to their undefinable simples.

Instead of answering the question, "What did I formerly believe myself to be?" with such answers as "a human" or "a rational animal," Descartes changes his strategy by listing the kinds of properties he had formerly attributed to himself:

In the first place, then, I considered myself as having a face, hands, arms, and all that system of members composed of bones and flesh as seen in a corpse which I designated by the name of body. *In addition to this I considered that I was nourished, that I walked, that I felt, and that I thought, and I referred all these actions to the soul*: but I did not stop to consider what the soul was, or if I did stop, I imagined that it was something extremely rare and subtle like a wind, a flame, or an ether, which was spread throughout my grosser parts. As to body I had no manner of doubt about its nature, but thought I had a very clear knowledge of it; and if I had desired to explain it according to the notions that I had then formed of it, I should have described it thus: By the body I understand all that which can be defined by a certain figure: something which can be confined in a certain place, and which can fill a given space in such a way that every other body will be excluded from it; which can be perceived either by touch, or by sight, or by hearing, or by taste, or by smell: which can be moved in many ways not, in truth, by itself, but by something which is foreign to it, by which it is touched [and from which it receives impressions]: for to have the power of self-movement, as also of feeling or of thinking, I did not consider to appertain to the nature of body: on the contrary, I was rather astonished to find that faculties similar to them existed in some bodies.[18]

This passage contains more than a list of the kinds of properties which Descartes claims he had, as an ordinary man prior to philosophizing, attributed to himself. He also in this passage presents the intellectually unsophisticated position (common sense) regarding the body and the soul and their relationship of which, I might add, Aristotelianism is a sophisticated version. Descartes begins by listing the parts of the body—hands, arms, legs, and so on—which belong to both a living body and a corpse, and the functions of the soul—nutrition, self-movement, motion, feeling, and thought—which belong to the living body but not to a corpse. The italicized sentence above brings out what is central to the common sense and Aristotelian approach to the soul; the soul is introduced as an explanatory hypothesis to account for the fact that some bodies have the power of self-movement, feeling, and thought, whereas others do not. In accordance with this common sense approach, there is no epistemological privilege respecting a person's knowledge of the existence of his own soul. I do not first know that I have a soul and then, as a result of observing that other organic bodies resemble my own, both in appearance and behavior, conclude that they too have souls. Not at all; I learn that I have a soul for the same reason; and at the same time, I learn that other human beings have souls.

Fundamentally, the common sense approach is no different in principle from that of a scientist who postulates the existence of subatomic particles in order to account for the observable behavior of light or gas. The soul is what, in present-day philosophy of science, is called a "theoretical entity" in that it is an unobservable, introduced for the purpose of explaining certain observable facts. Notice also that Descartes in the above passage includes nutrition and walking as activities of the soul. For common sense, as for Aristotle, the soul, so to speak, comes into the picture when we wish to explain the difference between the living and the nonliving bodies. Consequently, there is a continuity from the plant to the human. A plant manifests a life which is confined to nutrition, growth, and reproduction; and a primitive soul is therefore introduced as animating the body of the plant in order to account for these functions. An animal not only has the life functions of a plant but also sensation and self-movement, so that the soul of an animal is more complex than that of a plant. Finally, the human soul is the most complex of all, for the human not only has the functions of a plant and an animal but is capable of abstract thinking and reasoning as well.

Descartes' position, as we shall see, differs from this position on both counts. He rejects the notion of the soul, which he calls "the mind," as a theoretical entity and also rejects the doctrine that there is a continuity between the plant and the human. According to Descartes, the existence and nature of his mind (soul) becomes known to him as a result of reflecting on the "I" whose indubitable existence was established by the *Cogito* argument. This endeavor is precisely what he takes himself to be presently accomplishing in the *Second Meditation*. Moreover, as we shall see when we discuss Descartes' philosophy of nature, plants and animals are purely physical systems and are fundamentally no different from inorganic substances.

Descartes also claims that, prior to philosophizing, if he ever thought of what the soul might possibly be, he considered it to be some "rare" and "subtle" physical phenomenon. (This is neither the Aristotelian nor the Scholastic position.) This characterization of the soul was probably introduced by Descartes to indicate the ordinary man's allegiance to the senses; for, while the soul is not visible, he thinks that it must somehow resemble the things that are. Without explicitly criticizing the ordinary man's conception of the soul, Descartes implies that the ordinary man's state of mind is confused, for while he is convinced that bodies are incapable of initiating motion, he thinks of the soul as being composed of invisible rare and subtle bodies which, among other things, are supposed to explain self-movement.

Descartes goes on to show that he no longer has the right to be certain that he has either the body or the soul which he formerly attributed to himself:

But what am I, now that I suppose that there is a certain genius which is extremely powerful, and, if I may say so, malicious, who employs all his powers in deceiving me? Can I affirm that I possess the least of all those things which I have just said pertain to the

nature of the body? I pause to consider, I resolve all these th.
in my mind, and I find none of which I can say that it pertains to
me. It would be tedious to stop to enumerate them. Let us pass
to the attributes of soul and see if there is any one which is in me?
What of nutrition or walking [the first mentioned]? But if it is so
that I have no body, it is also true that I can neither walk nor take
nourishment. Another attribute is sensation. [The term "sensation"
and "feel" in this passage signifies a necessary reference to the body
and not in the more restricted way that Descartes later uses these
terms to signify mental occurrences without any necessary reference
to the body.] But one cannot feel without body, and besides I have
thought I perceived many things during sleep that I recognized in
my waking moments as not having been experienced at all. What
of thinking? I find here that thought is an attribute that belongs
to me; it alone cannot be separated from me. I am; I exist; that is
certain. But how often? Just when I think; for it might possibly
be the case if I ceased entirely to think, that I should likewise cease
altogether to exist. I do not now admit anything which is not necessarily true: to speak accurately I am not more than a thing which
thinks, that is to say a mind or a soul, or an understanding, or a
reason, which are terms whose significance was formerly unknown
to me. I am, however, a real thing and really exist; but what thing?
I have answered: a thing which thinks.[19]

Descartes uses the term "thought" very broadly. Since such
radically different items as a feeling of pain, the entertainment
of a concept, and a desire, are all thoughts, there is a temptation
to believe that Descartes identified thought with consciousness.
But this, as Robert McRae correctly argues, is a mistake: "For
Descartes, what I am conscious of, is what exists in me. What
I am thinking, i.e. what I am doubting, affirming, denying,
imagining, perceiving or feeling, when I am thinking of 'the
heavens, the earth, colours, figures, sound and all other external
things' are plainly not what exists in me."[20] We cannot, however,
have thoughts without being conscious of them. I cannot have
a feeling of pain or entertain the concept of a square without
being conscious of it. I need not necessarily attend to what
I am conscious of. I can have a feeling of pain and concentrate
my mind on Socrates' speech in the *Apology*. Second, when
Descartes says "I am a thing which thinks," we must not take
him to be claiming that the mind consists only of thoughts.

...hings which are innate in the mind but which ... aware of. The idol worshipper, for instance, ...d of the true God, has, as do all men, a concept ...f an absolutely perfect being, but since he has ...onscious of this concept in himself, he has never ...ght of God. And, third, what is most significant at this ... of Descartes' meditations, is that he absolutely can never doubt what he is conscious of in himself. For, even though he were always asleep and even though a demon were always deceiving him, he can say with complete assurance, "For it is so evident of itself that it is I who doubts, who understands and who desires, that there is no reason here to add anything to explain it."[21] Descartes expresses this insight with the words *Sum res cogitans* ("I am a thing which thinks").

The question which at once emerges is whether Descartes at this stage of his inquiry has demonstrated that the mind which is a thing that thinks can exist independent of the body. Or, to put this problem in sharper focus, Does the *Cogito* argument, once its implications are fully understood, provide Descartes with a clear and distinct idea of the mind as a substance distinct from that of the body? The answer to this question in both the *Discourse* and the *Search after Truth* is clearly in the affirmative. In the latter work, Descartes has Polyander say (with the approval of Eudoxus who represents Descartes), "Yet, while entirely setting aside all these suppositions, this will not prevent my being certain that I exist. On the contrary, they confirm me yet more in the certainty that I exist and that *I am not a body*; otherwise, doubting of my body I should at the same time doubt of myself, and this I cannot do; for I am absolutely convinced that I exist, and I am so much convinced of it, that I can in no wise doubt of it."[22] Descartes' argument (as voiced by Polyander) has the following form:

— (1) I can doubt that I have a body;

— (2) I cannot doubt that I exist;

— (3) hence, I and my body are not identical.

The principle Descartes needs for the validity of this argument is that, if two things are identical, then what is true of the one is necessarily true of the other. Now, since, by this argument, it is true of my body that I can doubt its existence but not true of myself, I and my body are distinct. But, unfortunately, this principle does not apply to intentional contexts such as desiring, worshipping, believing, and so on. For instance, an ambassador, on meeting Gerald Ford, might, by employing Descartes' kind of argument, arrive at the false conclusion that Ford is not from Grand Rapids, Michigan. He would reason as follows: "I cannot doubt that this man in front of me is the president of the United States, but I can doubt that he comes from Grand Rapids, Michigan; hence, I conclude that the president of the United States does not come from Grand Rapids, Michigan." The ambassador's argument is a poor one as is Descartes', since both arguments are similar in form.

Unlike in the *Discourse* and in the *Search after Truth*, Descartes denied, in the *Meditations*, that, in having established that he is a thing which thinks as the result of the *Cogito* argument, he had also established that he could exist without a body. He cannot be certain, he says, at this stage of his inquiry, that the "I" whose existence he cannot doubt is not identical with the body whose existence he can doubt: "But perhaps it is true that these same things which I suppose were non-existent [the matters pertaining to his body] because they are unknown to me, are really not different from the self which I know. I am not sure about this; I shall not dispute about it now; I can only give judgment on things that are known to me."[23]

Now, since Descartes considered the *Meditations* his most authoritative work and since it is the work in which he was most careful to follow the analytic method of discovery and to take nothing for granted, it would seem that we ought to give some weight, despite his argument in the *Search after Truth*, to the opinion that Descartes did not believe that the *Cogito* argument established the mind-body distinction. Moreover, Descartes continually referred his critics to the passage quoted above that, in the *Second Meditation*, he did not contend that, as a thinking substance, he could exist without a body. In a letter to Mersenne, Descartes writes: "You should not find it strange, either, that I do not prove in my *Second Meditation* that the soul is really distinct from the body, but merely show how to conceive it without the body. This is because I do not yet have, at that point, the premises needed for the conclusion. You find it later on, in the *Sixth Meditation*."[24]

Granted that Descartes did not claim to have established the mind-body distinction in the *Second Meditation*, did he believe, however, that he had there demonstrated that thought is his essence or, as he sometimes calls it, "the leading attribute"? "Essence" and "leading attribute" are technical terms and their meaning can be made clear by reference to Descartes' approach to the nature of substance. A substance, for Descartes, has two characteristics: first, it is the subject to which we attribute states, acts, qualities; second, a substance does not depend for its existence on anything else. Strictly speaking, only God is a substance, for He alone satisfies the second condition. Descartes allowed, however, that created things can be said to be substances, insofar as they depend *only* on God for their existence. Substance is therefore "a name which we cannot attribute in the same sense to God and His creatures."[25] The thing that concerns us at present is Descartes' belief that each substance has a principal attribute. The clearest and most detailed statement of his position is to be found in the *Principles*:

But although any one attribute is sufficient to give us a knowledge of substance, there is always one principal property of substance which constitutes its nature and essence, and on which all others depend. Thus extension in length, breadth and depth constitutes the nature of corporeal substance; and thought constitutes the nature of thinking substance. For all else that may be attributed to body presupposes extension, and is but a mode of this extended thing; as everything that we find in mind is but so many diverse forms of thinking. Thus, for example, we cannot conceive figure but as an extended thing, nor movement but as in an extended space; so imagination, feeling, and will, only exist in a thinking thing. But, on the other hand, we can conceive extension without figure or action, and thinking without imagination or sensation, and so on with the rest; as is quite clear to anyone who attends to the matter.[26]

Descartes does not identify substance with the leading attribute. When Descartes claims that his essence is thinking, the "I" and the thinking are distinct; thought belongs, or is predicated of, the self, but is not identical with it. For one thing, there are attributes such as unity and duration which are not derived from the essence. In an interview with Burman, Descartes says that substance is the unity of all its attributes: "All the attributes taken together are in truth the same thing as a substance; but not the attributes taken singly [this presumably would include the leading attribute] apart from the others."[27] There is, however, a passage in the *Principles* where Descartes appears to identify the substance with its leading attribute: "We may likewise consider thought and extension as constituting the natures of intelligence and corporeal substance; and then they must not be considered otherwise than as the very substances that think and are extended, i.e. as mind and body; for we know them in this way clearly and distinctly."[28]

For our purposes I don't think we have to take a stand on this issue for what concerns us at present is whether Descartes believed that his *Cogito* argument in the *Second Meditation* established that his essence is thinking. The evidence that he did is as follows. First, Descartes speaks of his thinking as the one and only attribute that is inseparable from his existence: "What of thinking? I find here that thought is an attribute that belongs to me, it alone cannot be separated from me."[29] Second, in the *Second Meditation*, Descartes states that the attributes of desiring, imagining, and feeling presuppose thinking but not the converse.[30] This way of drawing the distinction corresponds exactly with the manner in which in the above quotation from the *Principles* Descartes distinguished the leading attribute which is the essence of a substance from the others. Now, since Descartes, in the *Second Meditation*, noted that the other attributes are mere modes of thought, it would seem that already in the meditation Descartes identified his essence with thinking. Third, in his reply to one of Arnauld's criticisms, Descartes writes:

Consequently, if I had not been in search of certitude greater than the vulgar, I should have been satisfied with showing in the *Second Meditation* that *Mind* was apprehended as a thing that subsists, although nothing belonging to the body be ascribed to it. . . . And I should have added nothing more in order to prove that there was a real distinction between mind and body. . . . But, since one of these hyperbolical doubts adduced in the *First Meditation* went so far as to prevent me from being sure of this very fact (*viz*, that things are in their true nature exactly as we perceive them to be), so long as I supposed that I had no knowledge of the author of my being. . . .[31]

In this passage, Descartes is saying that he was not, in the *Second Meditation*, certain that he could exist as a mind without a body, because, in order to demonstrate this fact, he required as a premise "that things are in their true nature exactly as we perceive them to be." He could not, however, be certain of the truth of this premise until he discovered that a non-deceiving God is the "author of his being." This discovery he did not make until the *Third Meditation*. Prior to that *Meditation*, he could not be certain that a demon might not be deceiving him by making his thinking, which he cannot doubt, depend on the existence of his body, which he can. Notice that Descartes' reason for failing to make the body-mind distinction in the *Second Meditation* is not because he did not know that thought was his leading property but rather because he lacked God's guarantee that what is clearly and distinctly perceived is true.

I am inclined to think that the evidence favors the position that, in the *Second Meditation*, Descartes believed that he had already discovered that thinking was his leading attribute. We can reconstruct his position in our own words: "Thanks to the *Cogito* argument, I was able to distinguish myself as a thinking being from my body, and since I was certain that I existed as a thing that thinks, but doubtful of the existence of my body, I realized that if it were possible (it may not be possible) for my mind to exist without my body that would be sufficient for me to exist. And on the other hand, were I to cease to think, even if my body continued to exist, and even if it continued to undergo life functions such as nutrition and self-movement, I would cease to exist, I now see clearly and distinctly that thinking is both a necessary and sufficient condition for my existence; my having a body, even a biologically living one, is neither."

It seems that Descartes held that the above distinction between his body and his mind respecting his existence follows from the *Cogito* argument and that, consequently, he believed that he had discovered in the *Second Meditation* that thinking is his essence. The latter, however, does not entail that Descartes could possibly exist without a body. For it might be that thoughts are, as some contemporary philosophers believe, neurophysiological brain events and, in that case, if Descartes did not have a brain, which is part of his body, he could not exist. Descartes' insight, in my opinion, was not that body and mind are distinct substances but rather his conviction that, even if they were not, thought is nevertheless a person's leading attribute. The insight might be put in the following way (and here I am suggesting that in the *Second Meditation* Descartes anticipated Kant): the "I" who identifies himself as Descartes is a subject that thinks, but what this "I" is, is an open question; it might be a spiritual substance or a biological body or an aggregate of particles, and so on.

For the intellectual pilgrim of the *Meditations* who began from an unsophisticated common sense position about the nature of the world and himself, *Sum res cogitans* is the first clear and distinct idea which he had achieved. He was able to accomplish this feat by clearly distinguishing what there is about his nature which he can be absolutely certain about and what he cannot on the supposition that a demon is deceiving him. Also, as a result of obtaining this clear and distinct idea, he is now in the position for the first time to distinguish his faculty of the pure understanding from sensing and imagining. Thus our pilgrim has achieved one of Descartes' purposes for initiating skepticism, as he had related to Hobbes, namely, to acquire the ability to distinguish matters pertaining to the intellect from those of the senses. And also in *Sum res cogitans* he discovered the first principle, which was another reason for Descartes' initiating the skeptical venture, which constitutes the foundation for all the sciences. But, despite these accomplishments, which can be credited to Descartes' discovery, as the intellectual pilgrim, that he exists as a thinking thing, he has by no means discredited skepticism. At best, he has shown a limitation in trying to apply a skeptical attitude to all of one's beliefs. Skepticism is not eliminated, as was indicated

above, until a benevolent nondeceiving God replaces the demon
as the author of his being.

III *The Wax Experiment*

The famous wax experiment which immediately follows the
section *"Sum res cogitans"* in the *Second Meditation* is not
primarily intended by Descartes to present what he takes to
be a true scientific conception of the nature of body but rather
to reinforce the fact that his first principle of knowledge is
his existence as a thinking being and not the existence of corporeal bodies. This new section opens with the following words:

From this time I begin to know what I am with a little more clearness and distinction than before; but nevertheless it still seems to
me, and I cannot prevent myself from thinking, that corporeal things,
whose images are framed by thought, which are tested by the senses,
are much more distinctly known than that obscure part of me which
does not come under the imagination. Although really it is very
strange to say that I know and understand more distinctly these
things whose existence seems to me dubious which are unknown to
me, and which do not belong to me, than others of the truth of
which I am convinced, which are known to me and which pertain
to my real nature, in a word, than myself. But I see clearly how
the case stands: my mind loves to wander, and cannot yet suffer
itself to be retained within the just limits of truth. Very good, let
us once more give it the freest rein, so that, when afterwards, we
seize the proper occasion for pulling up, it may the more easily be
regulated and controlled.[32]

Immediately after proclaiming *"Sum res cogitans,"* Descartes
sensed a conflict within himself, as the above passage indicates,
between his reason and his natural tendency as a human being.
Reason has taught him that at present he has no right to be
absolutely certain about anything other than that he exists as a
thinking being; but on the other hand, his natural instinct, so
to speak, keeps prodding him that corporeal things which are
revealed to him by his senses are better known than his self
as a thinking thing which he can neither sense nor form an
image of. Descartes is here expressing his hesitancy in accepting
Sum res cogitans as the first principle of knowledge, despite

his conviction of the cogency of his former reasoning and despite his present state of doubting that corporeal bodies exist. He simply cannot as yet confine himself "within the just limits of truth." The passage quoted above clearly indicates that epistemological and psychological elements cannot be considered completely apart from each other in the *Meditations*.

From a purely epistemological point of view Descartes had no need for introducing this psychological tension within himself; he had merely to proceed to draw out the implications from the fact that he is a thinking being. This display of psychological tension is due to Descartes' conviction that demonstration and proof, if it is not to be thought of purely in an abstract fashion but in a concrete living context, cannot be completely divorced from the activity of persuasion. A person at any stage of inquiry has built in habits and prejudices, and a proof must encounter the person, to state it colloquially, at where he is. What we find in the passage quoted above is that Descartes, in the name of the natural light of reason, is trying to persuade Descartes, the natural man, and he does so by letting the natural man have his way. "Very good," he says, "let us once more give it the freest rein, so that, when afterwards we seize the proper occasion for pulling up, it may the more easily be regulated and controlled." He continues:

Let us begin by considering the commonest matters, those which we believe to be the most distinctly comprehended, to wit, the bodies which we touch and see; not indeed bodies in general, for these general ideas are usually a little more confused, but let us consider one body in particular. Let us take, for example, this piece of wax: it has been taken quite freshly from the hive, and it has not yet lost the sweetness of the honey which it contains; it still retains somewhat of the odour of the flowers from which it has been culled; its colour, its figure, its size are apparent; it is hard, cold, easily handled, and if you strike it with the finger, it will emit a sound. Finally all the things which are requisite to cause us distinctly to recognize a body, are met with in it. But notice that while I speak and approach the fire what remained of the taste is exhaled, the smell evaporates, the colour alters, the figure is destroyed, the size increases, it becomes liquid, it heats, scarcely can one handle it, and when one strikes it, no sound is emitted. Does the same wax remain after this change? We must confess that it remains; none would judge otherwise. What then did I know so distinctly in this piece of wax? It could certainly be nothing of all that the senses brought to my notice, since all these things which fall under taste, smell, sight, touch, and hearing are found to be changed, and yet the same wax remains.[33]

Descartes raises the question, "Does the same wax remain after this change"? And his answer, "We must confess that it remains," is ambiguous. We can, with respect to a piece of wax, refer to three different things: (1) the wax as a material body; that is to say, the respects in which wax does not differ from fire, wood, iron, water, but differs from minds; (2) the wax, insofar as it has certain characteristics by virtue of which it is called "wax." The characteristics in this case have to do with the powers of wax, its functions and uses. Wax has the power of making impressions and is useful as a seal. (3) The perceptible qualities of color, smell, shape, and so on, by which a body can be identified as wax.

Now, when Descartes speaks of the piece of wax remaining the same after being exposed to heat, he could mean either (1) or (2). He could mean the continuity of the existence of the wax as a body or its continuity as wax. It is unlikely that he meant (2). True, a body may, as a result of heating, lose *some* of its perceptible qualities by which it was identified as wax and still remain wax because its powers and uses have remained the same. But what is not possible is that *all* its perceptible qualities be changed and it remain wax. In this case, when Descartes asked, Does the same wax remain after the change, the proper answer should have been No, for it is no longer wax. I take it, then, that Descartes had (1) in mind. He was concerned not with the continuity of the wax's existence as wax but with its continuity as a physical body. There is no doubt that there is continuity in this latter sense, for we should sometimes want to say "this body at one time was wax but is now no longer wax." Descartes' claim that he is not dealing with "bodies in general" but one body in particular is, therefore, if my clarification of the ambiguity is correct, misleading. For he is dealing with "bodies in general," and the fact that he is employing a particular piece of wax to illustrate the points of his argument makes his study no less an inquiry into the abstract nature of bodies.

Descartes contends that what accounts for the continuity of the existence of the wax as body is "nothing of all that the senses brought to my notice, since all these things which fall under taste, smell, sight, touch, and hearing, are found to be changed, and yet the same wax remains." Descartes seems to imply that the continuity of a body's existence necessitates there being at least one property of the body which remains the same throughout its history. This is a questionable assumption. I have no doubt that, in order for a body to remain as wax over a period of time, it must possess at least one property which remains the same throughout the period, but I am by no means certain that this is true of a body *qua* body. It seems to me perfectly meaningful to say, "this body's properties have all changed, not merely its perceptible ones, but it is the same identical body as before." I am inclined to believe that the continuity of a body *qua* body does not have to do with its properties which make it the sort of body it is but with its location and continuity in space.

Having denied that the perceptible qualities account for the continuity of the existence of the wax as a body, Descartes continues with his argument:

Perhaps it was what I now think, *viz.* that this wax was not that sweetness of honey, nor that agreeable scent of flowers, nor that particular whiteness, nor that figure, nor that sound, but simply a body which a little while before appeared to me as perceptible under these forms, and which is now perceptible under others. But what precisely, is it that I imagine when I form such conceptions? Let us attentively consider this, and abstracting from all that does not belong to the wax, let us see what remains. Certainly nothing remains excepting a certain extended thing which is flexible and moveable.[34]

Descartes does not, in my opinion, clearly distinguish two different problems: (1) what constitutes the continuity of a body *qua* body? In other words, why does a body retain its identity despite the fact that all its properties have changed?; and (2) what characteristics must be true of all bodies insofar as they are bodies? The two questions, though related, are distinct, for the answer to one is not necessarily an answer to the other. Descartes began "the wax experiment" by raising the first problem, but in the passage above he seems to have shifted his interest to the second one.

What must be true of a body insofar as it is a body? Descartes' answer is that it must be a "certain extended thing which is flexible and moveable." Why did he confine the essential properties of a body to these two characteristics? Surely his reason could not have been because the wax had changed what would appear to be its other properties such as color and smell. For being flexible, it also changed its figure and, being moveable, was stationary before, but is now in motion. Why should he not have concluded that a body must have some color or other as well as being flexible and moveable? I think the key to understanding Descartes' argument is the word "perhaps" with which he began the above quotation. The burning of the wax and Descartes' noticing that all its perceptible qualities have changed are merely ways of preparing the reader, and himself as a philosophical novice, for entertaining the possibility (not demonstrating the fact) that color, sound, and smell are not properties of bodies but perceptual cues by which they are identified. In this manner, Descartes is able to prepare the reader for the contemplation of a body clearly and distinctly. The contemplation is guided by the question: what is essential for some X's being a body and what is nonessential? And Descartes' answer is that necessarily X must be an extended thing which is flexible and moveable but need not have some determinate color, smell, or sound.

But it is apparent, from what Descartes says following the above discovery, that his prime intent in "performing the wax experiment" is to conclude that the perception of a body is not the result of vision or the imagination, but of the understanding:

But what is the meaning of flexible and moveable? Is it not that I imagine that this piece of wax being round is capable of becoming square and of passing from a square to a triangular figure? No, certainly it is not that, since I imagine it admits of an infinitude of similar changes, and I nevertheless do not know how to compass the infinitude by my imagination, and consequently this conception which I have of the wax is not brought about by the faculty of imagination. What now is this extension? Is it not also unknown? For it becomes greater when the wax is melted, greater when it is boiled, and greater still when the heat increases; and I should not conceive [clearly] according to truth what wax is, if I did not think that even this piece that we are considering is capable of receiving more variations in extension than I have ever imagined. We must then grant that I could not even understand through the imagination what this piece of wax is, and that it is my mind alone which perceives it. I say this piece of wax in particular, for as to wax in general it is yet clearer. But what is this piece of wax which cannot be understood excepting by the [understanding or] mind? It is certainly the same that I see, touch, imagine, and finally is the same which I have always believed it to be from the beginning. But what must particularly be observed is that its perception is neither an act of vision, nor of touch, nor of imagination, and has never been such although it may have appeared formerly to be so, but only an intuition of the mind, which may be imperfect and confused as it was formerly, or clear and distinct as it is at present, according as my attention is more or less directed to the elements which are found in it, and of which it is composed.[35]

Descartes considers that he had already demonstrated, when observing the continuity of the existence of the wax, despite the fact that all its perceptual qualities have changed, that the perception of the body and its continuity was not the result of vision, smell, or sound. He argues that the perception cannot be the result of the imagination either. Why not? Because, in having a conception of flexibility, one can conceive the wax taking on any number of an infinite number of possible shapes, but one can only form a limited finite number of images. He makes a similar point about extension. Notice also that near the end of the above quotation, Descartes is saying that, whether the perception of the wax is clear and distinct as it presently is, or confused as it formerly was, in any case the perception is an act of the understanding and not of vision, touch, or the imagination. He is not, however, denying that the latter may be involved in the perception of the wax; his point is rather that the perception, even if confused, is not to be identified with vision, touch, or imagining. Vision and touch, however, may

activate the understanding and provide cues for the intuition
of the mind. For it is by means of color, smell, figure, and so
on that I judge the presence of a body and identify it to be
of a certain sort.

Descartes encounters a new obstacle to his position. Perceptual verbs such as "see," "hear," "smell," and "touch" seem
to imply that it is by means of the senses that we obtain knowledge of physical bodies. I say "I see the same wax" and not
"I judge it to be the same wax from its having the same figure
and color." From this way of speaking, it would appear that
it is by means of vision and not by the understanding that I
know it to be the same wax. But (says Descartes) this is really
no obstacle to his position if we bear in mind the following fact:

> ... When looking from a window and saying, "I see men who pass
> in the street," I really do not see them, but *infer* that what I see is
> men, just as I say that I see wax. And yet what do I see from the
> window but hats and coats which may cover automatic machines?
> Yet I judge these to be men. And similarly, solely by the faculty of
> judgment which rests in my mind, I comprehend that which I be-
> lieved I saw with my eyes.[36]

Descartes is here drawing the following analogy: (1) I see
a certain color and figure and infer that it is wax; and (2) I see
the hats and coats and infer that they are being worn by men.

The analogy is a poor one. In the first place, if Descartes'
position is correct, we do not see hats and coats but judge
that there are hats and coats present. For, just as I judge X
to be wax, in the same way I judge Y to be a hat. Second, I
not only judge the body to be wax; but, as Descartes says,
there is an act of the understanding by which I perceive it
to be wax. There is no perception of the understanding involved in the case of the hats and the coats. I merely judge
from their presence that they are being worn by men. And
third, I can see (using "see" in the ordinary sense) the men
without their hats and coats, and the hats and coats without
the men; but I cannot see the wax without its having some
color or figure or the latter without its being the color or figure
of some sort of object, whether it be wax, copper, or wood.

I suspect, however, that, despite Descartes' use of the analogy, the point he wished to make was not that the two cases are very similar, but rather that, because ordinary language is clearly shown to be unreliable in the case of the hats and coats, we have no reason to rely on it in the case of the wax. In ordinary language, says Descartes, I say, "I see the men," when, even if ordinary language was right about perceptual verbs, I only see the hats and coats. Why, then, should I take as a criticism of my position the fact that, in ordinary language I say "I see the wax" rather than "I judge this to be wax." A bit of evidence for my interpretation is that, immediately after the above quotation, Descartes says, "a man who makes it his aim to raise his knowledge above the common should be ashamed to derive the occasion for doubting from the forms of speech invented by the vulgar."

Descartes introduced the wax experiment in order to remove a psychological obstacle for his accepting *Sum res cogitans* as the first principle of knowledge. Once it was concluded, he felt that this obstacle had been removed:

But finally here I am, having insensibly reverted to the point I desired, for, since it is now manifest to me that even bodies are not properly speaking known by the sense or by the faculty of imagination, but by the understanding only, and since they are not known from the fact that they are seen or touched, but only because they are understood, I see clearly that there is nothing which is easier for me to know than my mind.[37]

CHAPTER 5

Reason

IT has now been shown that Descartes made two discoveries. The first was that, even when he thought that an all-powerful demon was deceiving him, he could not doubt that he existed as a being that thinks. And the second was that he possessed a faculty of reason (the understanding) by which he was able clearly and distinctly to perceive things, and which was distinct from sense, memory, and imagination. His discovery of these two facts had a significant impact on his skepticism. As before, he continued to think that a demon was deceiving him and that in reality there was no earth or sky or any other object, including his own body, which he *seemed* to perceive by his senses; but now a new element had, so to speak, entered the picture, namely, clear and distinct perception. If the demon is all-powerful, as he is alleged to be, declares Descartes, then no doubt he has the ability to deceive Descartes, even with regard to what he clearly and distinctly perceives; but, on the other hand, how could Descartes possibly be mistaken with regard to this mode of perception. This is an issue which Descartes took a stand on even before he attempted to demonstrate the existence of a benevolent God. It is a difficult and complicated subject. Moreover, Cartesian scholars are very much in disagreement about it. Nevertheless, we cannot evade considering the matter if we are to understand and appreciate the role that God plays in Descartes' philosophy.

Descartes became aware of the principle that what is clearly and distinctly perceived is true, shortly after his discovery of *Sum res cogitans.* "I am certain," he writes, "that I am a thing which thinks; but do I not then likewise know what is requisite to render me certain of a truth? Certainly in this first knowledge there is nothing that assures me of its truth, excepting

the clear and distinct perception of that which I state..."[1]
Notice that Descartes does not conclude that he exists as a
thinking substance because of his conviction that what is
clearly and distinctly perceived is true; rather he is first convinced that he existed as a thinking being and then, reflecting
on what has made him certain of this, he discovered that it is
because he clearly and distinctly perceived it to be true. Descartes' position in this matter is the same as that of Spinoza,
who held "a true idea as the standard of truth."[2] Spinoza meant
by this, first, that one cannot discover the standard for knowledge without first being in possession of an instance of
knowledge; and second, that any instance of knowledge can
serve as the basis for discovering the standard.

I *Skepticism of Reason*

After Descartes discovered the criterion of knowledge, he
writes the following unusual statement which has puzzled his
commentators:

But every time that this preconceived opinion of the sovereign power
of a God [the demon] presents itself to my thought, I am constrained to confess that *it is easy for him, if he wishes it, to cause me
to err, even in matters in which I believe myself to have the best
evidence.* And, on the other hand, always when I direct my attention
to things which I believe myself to perceive very clearly, *I am so
persuaded of their truth* that I let myself break out into words such
as these: Let who will deceive me, he can never cause me to be
nothing while I think that I am, or some day cause it to be true to
say that I have never been, it being true now to say that I am, or
that two and three make more or less than five, or any such thing
in which I see a manifest contradiction.[3]

Descartes seems to hold two contradictory propositions here.
And, if we keep in mind, Descartes' position that, prior to his
being justifiably certain that God exists, he can seriously entertain the possibility that a wicked all-powerful demon is trying
to deceive him on all matters, we can formulate the apparent
conflict of the two propositions as follows: (1) whether I know
or do not know that a benevolent God exists, whenever I clearly

and distinctly perceive something, I know it to be true; and (2) prior to knowing that a benevolent God exists I can doubt that what is clear and evident to me is true. How can (1) and (2) be logically compatible? If Descartes knows many specific intuitions to be true prior to his knowledge that God exists, how can he doubt the reliability of his faculty of reason; and, conversely, if he doubts its reliability, how can he accept its pronouncements to be true?

One interpretation of the passage quoted above, which has been adopted by a number of Descartes' commentators, is that he is not contradicting himself. They argue that he never held (1) above but rather (1)' as follows: (1)' whether I know or do not know that a benevolent God exists, whenever I clearly and distinctly perceive something, I cannot help but have the feeling of certainty that it is true. Propositions (1) and (1)' are not identical, for the former (in which "know" is being used in the strict and proper philosophical sense) involves metaphysical certainty and the latter psychological certainty. This point is clearly stated by Alan Gewirth:

Descartes has thus indicated a distinction between two kinds of certainty, the one psychological, in which the mind is compelled to assent to the truth of directly present clear and distinct perceptions, but in which metaphysical doubt is still possible; and the other metaphysical, in which the mind is so assured of the truth of clear and distinct perceptions that even metaphysical doubt is impossible.[4]

In a similar vein, Harry Frankfurt writes that it is an "erroneous notion that whenever Descartes says that something is indubitable, that is tantamount to his saying that it is true." In a further passage referring to Descartes' insistence that he cannot doubt present intuitions, Frankfurt writes: "... Descartes describes the convictions he is irresistibly inclined to hold under certain circumstances, and he reports the assertions he feels urgently moved under these circumstances to make. But he does not say either that the convictions are reasonable or that the assertions are true."[5]

This position which Gewirth and Frankfurt attribute to Descartes is not meaningful. Furthermore I doubt that Descartes ever held it. It seems to me that there can be no distinction between a person's psychological state of being certain that p (where p stands for some proposition) is true from his possessing an unqualified commitment to the truth of p. Consequently, a person cannot logically report about "the assertions he feels urgently moved to make" without his saying or implying that "the convictions are reasonable" and "the assertions are true." What I am claiming is reflected in the difference between first-person present-tense uses of terms like "indubitable," "certain," and "doubt" and their uses in other tenses. The sentence "Can I doubt p?" unlike "Did I doubt p?" is synonymous with the sentence "Is p true?" because a person cannot possibly be in the state of trying to determine whether he doubts p without deliberating as to whether p is true. It is meaningful to say "p *was* indubitable to me but it may be false"; but not "p *is* indubitable to me but it may be false." When a person says that he cannot doubt p, he is not reporting the condition of his mind except incidentally, nor is he saying or implying that because he cannot doubt p, p is true; the very point of his remark is that because p is true, he cannot doubt it. If, in fact, he thought that perhaps the reason p is indubitable to him is that he has a certain psychological make-up which determines him to believe p, he would, as a consequence of this reflection, immediately doubt p. For no man, unless he has Godlike pretentions, believes that his feelings of certainty constitute an adequate criterion for knowledge.

There is an alternative to attributing to Descartes a contradiction or a meaningless distinction. When Descartes, in the first half of the above passage, says that a wicked God might be deceiving him, even respecting what is clearly and distinctly perceived, his statement is ambiguous. It might mean (1) he doubts the truth of the principle "that whatever is clearly and distinctly perceived is true"; or (2) he doubts the truth of such statements as "two and three make five" or "whatever is once done cannot be undone." I believe that, whenever Descartes speaks of doubting what is clear and evident, he is asserting (1), whereas when he claims, as he does in the second half of the above passage, that he cannot doubt what he intuits, he is denying (2). What is involved here is not, as Gewirth and Frankfurt think, two different uses of the term "doubt" but rather two different intentional objects of doubt. That Descartes need not be contradicting himself can be seen in the following way. Suppose that at time T_1 Descartes intuits that two and three make five; but subsequently at T_2, thinking that a demon might be deceiving him even respecting those matters which are clear and evident to him, he comes to doubt that what he intuited at T_1 is true. It does not follow that at T_2 Descartes doubts that two and three make five. On the contrary, given Descartes' position that what is clearly and distinctly perceived cannot be doubted, a necessary condition that he doubt that what he intuited at T_1 is true is that he not remember that what he had intuited was that two and three make five. Descartes can, with good reason, doubt the principle "that what is clearly and distinctly perceived is true." He can do so, because an all-powerful demon undoubtedly could have created him with faculties, including his understanding, which are completely defective. But no demon, even if he were all-powerful, could bring it about that two and three are more or less than five or that what is once done can be undone. It is Descartes' conviction that the archdeceiver cannot bring about "a manifest contradiction" that makes it impossible for him to doubt his intuitions. It is not the psychological fact that he simply cannot help but believe what he clearly and distinctly perceives.

But, if Descartes cannot doubt what he intuits at the time that he intuits it, what need does he have of God's guarantee that his faculty of reason is not defective in order for him to possess scientific knowledge? No doubt Descartes needs God's guarantee in order to have knowledge about nature, for he does not even have an intuition that nature exists. But mathematical propositions, as noted previously, do not depend for their truth on the existence of the world and when clearly and distinctly perceived, are "seen" to be hypothetical. Why could not Descartes begin with mathematically self-evident truths, and then, by successive acts of intuition (what in the *Regulae* and elsewhere he called "deduction"), achieve a body of mathematical knowledge without the need of God's guarantee of the standard of knowledge? There can be no doubt, nevertheless, that Descartes held that God's guarantee is essential to any scientific knowledge including mathematics:

That an atheist can know clearly that the three angles of a triangle are equal to two right angles, I do not deny; I merely affirm that, on the other hand, such knowledge on his part cannot constitute true science, because no knowledge that can be rendered doubtful should be called science. Since he is, as supposed, an Atheist, he cannot be sure that he is not deceived in the things that seem most evident to him, as has been sufficiently shown; and though perchance the doubt does not occur to him, nevertheless it may come up, if he examine the matter, or if another suggests it; he can never be safe from it unless he first recognizes the existence of a God.[6]

There are two reasons Descartes gives for his need of God's guarantee, despite the fact that he cannot doubt what he intuits is true at the time that he intuits it. In the first place, occasionally he employs a long chain of reasoning, and though he intuits each and every step in the argument, he cannot take in, despite his use of the method of enumeration, all the steps, so to speak, in a single intuitive glance. Consequently, he can come to doubt the conclusion of the argument on the ground that his faculty of reason is defective. And, in order to eliminate the reasonableness of such doubt, he requires certain knowledge that God exists and that he can therefore be secure that whatever he intuits is true. Second, Descartes had often intuited the conclusion of an argument which he had made in the past, but now because he is not attending to the steps of the proof he only remembers that he perceived it clearly. He can then become skeptical about its truth, since he cannot be certain (his faculty of reason may be defective) that what he clearly and distinctly perceives is true. If we keep this latter point in mind, it should be apparent why Descartes rejected the possibility that someone ignorant of God's existence can have scientific knowledge. For a necessary condition for scientific knowledge is that theorems (conclusions) proven in the past are accepted in order for them to serve as premises for proving still other theorems. And since, without the knowledge of God's existence, a person cannot be certain that any proposition he *previously* intuited is true, any conclusions deducible from it would be subject to doubt:

> For although I am of such a nature that as long as I understand anything very clearly and distinctly, I am naturally impelled to believe it to be true, yet because I am also of such a nature that I cannot have my mind constantly fixed on the same object in order to perceive it clearly, and *as I often recollect having formed a past judgment without at the same time properly recollecting the reasons that led me to make it,* it may happen meanwhile that other reasons present themselves to me, which would easily cause me to change my opinion, if I were ignorant of the facts of the existence of God, and thus I should have no true and certain knowledge, but only vague and vacillating opinions.[7]

Despite the fact that there is no support for it in the texts of Descartes' writings, I suspect there is still another reason which might have influenced him to adopt the position that knowledge of God's existence is required for the validity of the mathematical sciences. Unless Descartes knows that his faculty of reason is reliable, he cannot be certain that, in trying to acquire scientific knowledge, he may not at some time in the future intuit a proposition which is the contrary or the contradictory to one or more of those which he already accepts on the most solid grounds. He lacks the assurance that he cannot intuit two conflicting propositions. True, he is presently certain that whatever is once done cannot be undone, but how can he be certain that he cannot at some time in the future intuit a proposition which is incompatible with it. Scientific knowledge, according to Descartes, is an organized system of secure and reliable propositions; and in order to have this knowledge, a person must be certain that his most authoritative faculty, namely reason, when exercised properly, is infallible. This certainty he can only acquire once he knows that God exists and that God, being benevolent, will not deceive him.

II   *The Cartesian Circle*

The use of the knowledge of God's existence to validate the principle that what is clearly and distinctly perceived is true has exposed Descartes to the charge of reasoning in a circle, that is, the Cartesian circle. The first use of this criticism was made by Arnauld. Descartes' circular reasoning, according to Arnauld, is as follows:

... The only secure reason we have for believing that what we clearly and distinctly perceive is true, is the fact that God exists.

But we can be sure that God exists, only because we clearly and evidently perceive that; therefore prior to being certain that God exists, we should be certain that whatever we clearly and evidently perceive is true.[8]

Arnauld's charge would no doubt be correct if Descartes required the principle "whatever is clearly and distinctly perceived is true" as a premise in his argument for God's existence. To be sure, he did not, in his argument in the *Meditations*, state the principle as one of his premises, but its omission does not preclude its being a hidden premise for establishing his conclusion that God exists. I am inclined to believe that the principle is not required. Unquestionably, if the principle were not true, Descartes would have no right to be certain that God exists, but I do not see that it follows from this that he required the principle as a premise. When Darwin employed his senses to establish the theory of evolution, he did not require as a premise in his argument that his senses be reliable conveyors of information about occurrences in nature, though no doubt, if the latter were not true, he would have no right to his belief in evolution.

Descartes points out two facts about his position which, according to him, clearly shows that he did not argue in a circle. The first is that God's guarantee is not required for present intuitions, but only for remembered ones: "... When I said that *we could know nothing with certainty unless we were first aware that God existed,* I announced in express terms that I referred only to the science apprehending such conclusions *as can recur in memory without attending further to the proofs which led me to make them.*"[9]

Second, Descartes claims that, in the *Third Meditation*, where he first established God's existence, all the steps in his argument

were intuited simultaneously, so that God's existence cannot be
subject to that very type of doubt (doubt about all remembered
intuitions) which His existence is supposed to eliminate: "For
first, we are sure that God exists, because *we have attended to
the proofs that established this fact*; but afterwards it is enough
for us to remember that we have perceived something clearly, in
order to be sure that it is true; but this would not suffice unless
we knew that God existed and that he did not deceive us."[10]
But Descartes still seems to be exposed to criticism in this
matter. For, after establishing God's existence in the *Third
Meditation*, Descartes cannot forever after keep before his mind
the steps in his proof of God's existence. He has to think on
other things. Consequently, God's existence becomes a remembered intuition. But then, why should it not become subject
to doubt as are all remembered intuitions? The force of this
criticism can be seen in the following way. Descartes could
have established the principle that what he intuits is true from
any specific intuition. In point of fact, in both the *Discourse*
and the *Meditations*, Descartes became certain of the principle
as a result of reflecting on the fact that he could not doubt
that he exists as a thinking being. And it was only later when
he merely remembered that he had a clear and distinct perception of the truth of the principle that he began to doubt it
on the ground that an all-powerful demon could bring it about
that whatever he intuits is false. Why should the matter be
any different in the case of God's existence? After the *Third
Meditation*, Descartes only remembers that he had a clear
and distinct perception of the truth of the principle as a result
of having established God's existence. Why should he not then
doubt, for the same reason, the truth of the principle as he
did after the *Cogito*?

This criticism can be met in that there is a crucial difference
between any argument for the reliability of reason from a
source other than God's existence and an argument from God's
existence. Let us consider an instance of the former kind of
argument:

(1) two and three make five; and
(2) there is nothing that makes me certain of the truth of (1)
except that I clearly and distinctly perceive it. Hence:

(3) all things which I intuit are true (my faculty of reason is reliable).

This argument is not an instance for Descartes of formal reasoning. However, the certainty of the premises confers certainty to the conclusion despite the fact that the premises are about a specific kind of intuition, whereas the conclusion is about intuition in general. The important point to notice is that (2) is a premise which is absolutely essential for establishing the conclusion; for it is conceivable that Descartes might have intuited that two and three make four. The above argument, while it proves that his faculty of reason is reliable, does not demonstrate that this must necessarily be the case. It does not show the following proposition to be true:

(4) there is a necessary connection between my having a faculty of reason and my faculty's being reliable.

Consider now an argument which resembles the above one:

(1)′ a benevolent nondeceiving God exists; and

(2)′ there is nothing that makes me certain of the truth of (1)′ except that I clearly and distinctly perceive it. Hence:

(3)′ all things which I intuit are true.

In this argument, unlike the previous one, (2)′ is an unnecessary and superfluous premise because the truth of (3)′ follows directly from (1)′. A benevolent God necessarily would not allow Descartes to have a defective faculty. Moreover, Descartes, in his argument in the *Third Meditation*, tries to demonstrate that it is inconceivable that he exists and God does not. From these two facts, it follows that (4) is true.

In order to see how the distinction between these two arguments concerns the issue of remembered intuitions, it is important to remind ourselves of the nature of Cartesian methodological skepticism. Descartes held that a person ought to withhold assent from any statement if he can find even the slightest reason to doubt it. Prior to proving God's existence, Descartes does not know (4), namely, that there is a necessary connection between his having a faculty of reason and his faculty's being reliable; hence, he can entertain the possibility that a demon is deceiving him. This reflection constitutes a reason, in accordance with the procedure of methodological skepticism, for doubting all remembered intuitions, including his having in the past intuited that his faculty of reason is reliable. But once the existence of God is proved, Descartes knows (4) to be true; and since no demon can bring about "a manifest contradiction," he can no longer entertain the possibility that his faculty of reason is defective. Descartes thus no longer has a reason for doubting remembered intuitions, including the remembered intuition of God's existence.

CHAPTER 6

The First and Second Arguments for God's Existence

DESCARTES' discovery that he can doubt what he clearly and distinctly perceives is true led to the realization that his first and immediate priority should be to remove this doubt. True, the doubt is slight, he agrees, and since it is not grounded on an ample reason, it is, "so to speak, metaphysical." But since no organized body of knowledge is possible unless the doubt is removed, Descartes felt that he had to address himself immediately to this task. He must try to discover the ultimate source of his faculties: did they originate by chance or through the agency of some God; and if by a God, is He benevolent or malevolent? There was no other way, Descartes felt, by which he could ascertain whether his faculties, including the faculty of the understanding (reason), were reliable: "But in order to be able altogether to remove it [the doubt], I must inquire whether there is a God as soon as the occasion presents itself; and if I find that there is a God, I must also inquire whether He may be a deceiver; for without a knowledge of these two truths I do not see that I can ever be certain of anything."[1] Now, since Descartes has placed in doubt the physical world and other minds, and since the only thing he knows with absolute certainty to exist is himself as a thinking being, he has no recourse in conducting his inquiry but to examine the ideas which he finds in his mind. They appear to be of three kinds:

But among these ideas, some appear to me to be innate, some adventitious, and others to be formed [or invented] by myself; for, as I have the power of understanding what is called a thing, or a truth, or a thought, it appears to me that I hold this power from

117

no other source than my own nature [these are the innate ideas].
But if I now hear some sound, if I see the sun, or feel heat, I have
hitherto judged that these sensations proceeded from certain things
that exist outside of me [these are the adventitious ideas]; and
finally it appears to me that sirens and hippogryphs, and the like,
are formed out of my own mind. But again, I may possibly persuade
myself that all these ideas are of the nature of those which I term
adventitious, or else that they are all innate, or all fictitious: for
I have not yet clearly discovered their true origin.[2]

It is apparent from the last sentence that Descartes was not
presenting his position on the origin of ideas but rather on
how their origin appeared to him. He does not at present know
how his ideas originated; their origin is what he is trying
to find out. In a letter to Mersenne,[3] he presents the same
classification as that presented in the *Third Meditation*, but
with two notable differences. In the passage in the *Meditations*,
Descartes, under the heading of ideas constructed by the mind,
includes only fictional ones like that of a satyr and a hippo-
gryph, whereas, in his letter to Mersenne, he uses as his example
the astronomical conception of the sun which results from
reasoning. In both cases, the ideas are constructed. Fictitious
ideas are formed by the operation of the imagination in arbitrarily putting together certain adventitious ideas. On the other
hand, there are ideas formed by the mind, as in the case of the
astronomical idea of the sun, which result from the cooperation
of reason, the senses, and the imagination. A more significant
difference is the fact that in his letter, unlike in the passage
from the *Third Meditation*, Descartes identifies his innate ideas
with "true immutable and eternal essences." In the opening
to the *Third Meditation*, Descartes, following the methodical
order of discovery, has not yet realized that his innate ideas,
which are "eternal essences," and, as such, clear and distinct,
constitute the source from which he can totally liberate himself
from skepticism. This conclusion is apparent from the fact that,
at the outset, when he considers which among his ideas might
provide him with a reason to be certain that there exists something besides himself, he at first ignores his innate ideas and
confines his attention to his adventitious ones.

There are, contends Descartes, two possible reasons for concluding that adventitious ideas proceed from certain objects that are outside himself. The first is that he is taught this lesson by nature. He writes: "When I say that I am so instructed by nature, I merely mean a certain spontaneous inclination which impels me to believe in this connection . . ."[4] For instance, when Descartes perceives a luminous image, he spontaneously and, without reflection, is inclined to judge that there exists something external to his consciousness (the sun) which has caused him to have the image. Descartes rejects his natural impulse as providing a basis for an indubitable conviction that there exist objects external to his consciousness. The natural impulse must be distinguished from the natural light of reason. He observes, "But these two things are very different; for I cannot doubt that which the natural light causes me to believe to be true, as, for example, it has shown me that I am from the fact that I doubt, or other facts of the same kind."[5]

The other reason Descartes gives for possibly concluding that his adventitious ideas proceed from an external source is that they do not depend on his will and sometimes present themselves to his mind against his will. Descartes' example is, whether he wills or does not will, he feels heat and, consequently, is disposed to judge that this feeling is produced by something external to his mind, that is, by the heat of the fire near which he sits. And, again, this reason is not sufficient to convince him with an unquestionable certainty that there exists something besides himself. For there may be, for all he knows, a faculty within himself suitable to produce these ideas without the assistance of external objects. Besides, dream images do not appear as the result of the command of his will, but are, nevertheless, not due to the impact of external bodies on his senses.

Descartes next points out that, even if his adventitious ideas are produced by external objects, he has no reason for believing that his ideas resemble the objects which produce them. "On the contrary," says Descartes, "I have noticed that in many cases there was a great difference between the object and its idea." For example, there are two different ideas of the sun. The first is derived from the senses and is adventitious, and the other is the astronomical conception of the sun. The

two ideas of the sun are very different. The sensory image of
the sun is very small, whereas the astronomer's conception of
the sun is that of a body that is many times larger than the
earth. "These two ideas cannot, indeed, both resemble the
same sun," says Descartes, "and reason makes me believe that
the one which seems to have originated directly from the sun
itself, is the one which is most dissimilar to it."[6]

Descartes does not explain, in the passage from the *Third
Meditation*, what innate ideas are. There are, however, references to innate ideas in all of his later works, including his
letters. Unfortunately, he does not always use the term in the
same way. For example, in the *Notes Against a Programme*,[7]
he claims that all our ideas are innate on the ground that, even
in the case of sense perception, our ideas are formed by an
innate faculty of mind. For instance, my idea of the pen with
which at present I am writing is that of a substance which,
among other things, possesses color and smell. Given the fact
that the real pen has no such properties, my mind could not
have merely passively registered the stimuli provided by the
impact of the foreign body of the pen on my fingers. But, on
the contrary, the inner faculty of my mind, on the occasion
of the stimuli, created the idea which, prior to the study of
philosophy, I thought resembled the pen. Now, since the mind
not only with regard to intellectual matters, but, as in the
above illustration, in sensory matters as well, creates its ideas,
they are innate in the sense of, so to speak, being all native
to the mind and not brought in from the outside.

This use of "innate ideas," however, is confined to a passage
in the *Notes*. In his most prevalent use of the term, he distinguishes, as he did in the *Third Meditation*, innate ideas from
other kinds of ideas. But, even in these cases, he uses the
term in a variety of ways.

He often uses it to signify the mind's original programming.
He does not, in this sense, mean that infants are born entertaining in their minds such ideas as God, triangle, truth, and so on.
Nevertheless, by calling these ideas innate, Descartes indicates
that they are in some sense implicit in the infant's mind. In a
letter to Hyperaspistes, Descartes writes: "Nonetheless, it [the
infant] has in itself the ideas of God, itself and all such truths

as are called self-evident, in the same way as adult humans have when they are not attending to them."[8] And in the same letter he writes: "I do not doubt that all have within themselves at least an implicit idea of God, that is to say, an aptitude to perceive it explicitly; but I am not surprised that they do not feel themselves to have it, or do not notice that they have it, and perhaps will not notice it even after the thousandth reading of my meditations."[9] Perhaps the best way to understand what Descartes most often means when he uses the term "innate ideas" is to think of these ideas as analogous to the mind's logical programming. An infant's mind is born programmed with the valid rules of logic. Consider as an example the valid rule, *modus ponens*. Let P and Q stand for variables which can be replaced by sentences, the rule states that, if P then Q is true and P is true, then it follows that Q is also true. We know that we are programmed with this rule because young children, who have never studied logic and have never entertained the rule, when given an argument in which the variables above are replaced by actual sentences, are able to intuit the validity of the argument. Descartes' position is that, besides the formal rules of logic, our minds are programmed with the eternal truths. Were this not the case, we could not have intuitions of a nonformal nature. Unless a person was programmed with the eternal truth that "if something exists then it is either a mode of a substance or a substance," he could not, from the fact that he thinks, intuit that he must exist. Moreover, since our minds are programmed with eternal truths, we can correctly speak of certain ideas existing in the mind of an infant at birth. This assertion is so because the eternal truths, not being purely formal, must contain concepts which, though highly abstract, have material content. For instance, my mind is programmed with the eternal truth, "Whatever comes into existence must have been brought into existence by something else." We have in this formulation the ideas of existence, event, duration, nonexistence, cause, and plurality. Now, just as when a student studies logic, he is being instructed on the nature of his formal programming, in the same way Descartes' *Meditations* is largely, though by no means exclusively, an attempt by Descartes to discover his nonformal programming. Whether the human programming is defective or, on the contrary, an enabling condition for knowledge, is precisely what Descartes is presently, in the *Third Meditation,* investigating. Descartes, as we shall shortly see, discovers not only that the idea of God is part of his initial programming but also that God, operating through secondary causes such as his parents, is the programmer.

Another use of the term in the *Third Meditation* involves such ideas as substance, identity, perception, cause, reason, and many others, which the mind does not derive from the senses but from reflecting on the activity of its own thinking. True, I am directly aware of corporeal images, but I do not, and cannot, derive the notion of substance from reflecting on their nature. I derive it from being conscious of myself in the activity of thinking. And I derive my idea of causality when I reflect on the fact that a thought has occurred as the result of my having willed it. Once I derive such ideas as substance and causality from my own case, I then apply it to external phenomena. Ideas such as thought, substance, duration, number, are innate in the sense that every human has implicit knowledge of these concepts when he thinks about anything and can become aware of them when he reflects on his thinking.[10]

These are the three uses which Descartes made of the term "innate ideas." The first is that of "innate" in the sense that all ideas, including those of sensory objects, are actively formed by the activity of the mind. The second is that of "innate" in the sense of the mind's initial programming, which is a necessary condition for the possibility of human knowledge. And the third is that of "innate" in the sense that there are certain ideas implicit in the activity of thinking which the mind can become aware of by self-reflection. These different uses of the term do not, in my opinion, commit Descartes to any inconsistencies.

I *The Objective Existence of Ideas*

The problem Descartes faces is to determine whether he can have any certain knowledge that there is at least one idea within his mind which has been brought about by some thing or person other than himself. At first, as we have seen, he considered what might appear to be the most promising candidate for this task, that is, his adventitious ideas. They turned out to be a disappointment. The adventitious ideas did not, with unquestionable certainty, reveal the existence of things external to his mind. For all that he presently knows, he is, as a being that thinks, the only thing that exists. To probe further into this matter, Descartes decides to change his strategy. At this point in his meditations he introduces the first of a series of premises from which the conclusion "God exists" is derived. These premises must be considered in detail, not only because they are essential for Descartes' first argument for God's existence but also because they are central ideas in Descartes' philosophy in general. Descartes, in the following passage, describes his new strategy:

But there is yet another method of inquiring whether any of the objects of which I have ideas within me exist outside of me. If ideas are only taken as certain modes of thought, I recognize amongst them no difference or inequality, and all appear to proceed from me in the same manner; but when we consider them as images, one representing one thing and the other another, it is clear that they are very different one from the other. There is no doubt that those which represent to me substances are something more, and contain so to speak more objective reality within them [that is to say, by representation participate in a higher degree of being or perfection] than those that simply represent modes or accidents; and that idea again by which I understand a supreme God, eternal, infinite [immutable], omniscient, omnipotent, and Creator of all things which are outside of Himself, has certainly more objective reality in itself than those ideas by which finite substances are represented.[11]

Descartes is here distinguishing two aspects of an idea. The idea as an object or mode of the mind is the "formal reality" of the idea; and the idea, insofar as it represents something other than itself, is the "objective reality" of the idea. Thus, the ideas of God, triangle, and mountain are as formal realities the same, for all three are modes of the mind; but as objective realities they differ, for one represents God, another a triangle, and a third a mountain. Respecting this distinction, one must bear three things in mind. First, in order for the idea of X to represent Y, Y need not exist; the idea of a satyr represents a satyr, but there are no satyrs. Second, for the idea of X to represent Y, it need not resemble Y. The idea of God represents God but the idea has none of the properties of God; it is neither wise, powerful, or merciful, or so on. Third, for X to represent Y, it need not represent it clearly and distinctly. For instance, Jones' idea of clarity objectively represents clarity, but formally, it is a confused and unclear idea of clarity. As a result of considering ideas merely as formally existing in the mind, Descartes was able to demonstrate that he exists as a thing that thinks. This fact is apparent when one considers that, in the *Cogito* argument, what the idea represented was irrelevant respecting the use Descartes made of it to infer his existence. But he now hopes to discover that some thing or person exists besides himself by considering his ideas objectively, that is to say, in their representative capacity.

Descartes makes two other claims in the passage quoted above. The first is that different existent beings can be said to be more or less real; and, second, that this doctrine of degrees of reality applies to ideas not only as formal realities but as objective realities as well. Let us consider each of these claims. The doctrine of degrees of reality was accepted by the Scholastics. They thought of reality as a hierarchical system; the lowest reality is matter, the highest God; between them in the order of ascendency are plants, animals, men, and angels. It is debatable whether Descartes accepted the Scholastic position or radically revised it. If we accept the latter interpretation, then Descartes did not, for instance, believe that an angel has more reality than a man, and a man more than a worm. There are, according to this revision, only three degrees of reality: a finite substance, whether it is a thinking or a material substance, has a greater degree of reality than a mode; and God, in turn, as the infinite substance, has a greater degree of reality than both kinds of finite substances. The case for this interpretation is that, whenever Descartes explicitly states his position, as in the above passage and at the end of the second set of objections, he always confines his statement of it to a comparison of degrees of reality between mode, finite substance, and God.

Against this latter interpretation can be set two facts. First, later in the *Third Meditation* Descartes uses illustrations which are suitable to the Scholastic and not the revised version. And second, in replying to Caterus and to "divers theologians and philosophers" (the first and second set of objections), Descartes implies the Scholastic position. I am inclined to believe that Descartes' rejection of the Scholastic "hierarchy of being" also led to his radically revising their doctrine of degrees of reality. However, since Descartes believed that the argument for God's existence, which he is presenting in the *Third Meditation*, is a good argument on either the Scholastic or the revised version, he thought that, in addressing his audience and answering his critics, he could more effectively make his case by using examples they were familiar with and by not using his modified version as a premise in his argument.

The notion of degrees of reality is not, on the face of it, clear. Unfortunately, even when Hobbes prodded him—"Further I pray, M. Descartes to investigate the meaning of more reality"[12]— Descartes merely repeated what he had said in the *Meditations*. I think, however, that some light can be shed on what Descartes meant by degrees of reality if one thinks of *A* as having more reality than *B*, because *B* depends for its existence on *A*, but not *A* on *B*. A particular idea or act of will logically implies the existence of a mind, and it is in this sense that Descartes says that substance is more real than a mode. True, a substance can only exist insofar as it has modes, but it does not necessarily have to have the particular mode which it has in order to exist. For instance, my present sense impression cannot, in the logical sense of "cannot," exist without the existence of my mind, but I could exist without experiencing this particular impression. The relation, however, between finite substances and God appears to be very different from that between mode and substance. My mind and my body, as finite substances, are not predicated of God, in the sense in which a particular shape is predicated of my body and a particular feeling of my mind. I, and my body, may be dependent on God's existence in that, if God did not exist, neither my mind nor my body could exist. But the relation in this case is not that of predicate to subject but of effect to cause.

Descartes can meet this objection, because his position is that the causal relation between God and finite substances is not like that of oxygen and a flame, or that of heat and animal life. The fact that a flame depends for its existence on the presence of oxygen is a contingent fact, one which may have been otherwise. Possibly, there could have existed a world in which oxygen extinguishes rather than preserves a flame. On the other hand, the fact that finite substances depend for their existence on God is a necessary truth in that no substance can conceivably exist without the preserving creative activity of God. The dependence in this case involves both a causal and a logical relation. There is, therefore, a resemblance between a mode's dependence on a finite substance and the latter's dependence on God; for, in both cases, the order of dependence is logically necessary. Of course Descartes, at this stage, does not yet know that God exists. What he has the right to claim is that, if God exists, then whatever else exists necessarily depends for their continued existence on Him.

Descartes claims that not only does the doctrine of degrees of reality apply to modes, finite substances, and God, insofar as they exist formally but also as they exist objectively in the mind. Thus, not only is God superior to Socrates; but the idea of God, insofar as it represents God, is superior to the idea of Socrates, insofar as it represents Socrates. It makes no difference respecting what is involved here, whether what is represented by an idea exists or not. Zeus, the god of the ancient Greeks, has no formal, but only objective (existence in the mind) reality, but the idea of Zeus objectively has greater reality than the idea of motion; for motion is a mode of an extended substance whereas Zeus, if he existed, would be a finite substance.

Descartes' claim that ideas as objective realities possess degrees of reality distinct from their existence as modes of the mind puzzled his readers. Caterus could make no sense of it; for, as he says, "'objective reality' is a mere name and nothing actual."[13] What Caterus most likely meant by this latter remark (he never explained) is as follows: with respect to the distinction between formal and objective reality, words are analogous to ideas. The word "cow" in its formal reality is a mark on paper or a sound; and as in the case of an idea, we can distinguish its formal reality from its function as representing any cow. We might also, following Descartes, refer to the latter as "the objective reality of the word 'cow.'" There are, however, strictly speaking, only two realities involved here; there is the physical word "cow" and the person who uses the word to signify any cow. There is no third reality that somehow falls between the word and the person who employs it to which we can assign degrees of reality. It would clearly be absurd to say that the word "cow," because it represents a finite substance, has a lower degree of objective reality than the word "God" because it represents an infinite substance. The term "objective reality" is merely a way of talking. And, insofar as one speaks literally and strictly, an idea as a reality is a mere mode of the mind like the shape of a word is a mode of a body; and the fact that both represent things other than themselves does not involve any new realities which are named by the word "objective." I think in this matter Caterus is right.

Descartes' first argument for God's existence in the *Meditations* requires that an idea as objectively existing in the mind has a different degree of reality from its formal existence as a mode of the mind; and this is apparent in view of Descartes' argument that he does not have a sufficient degree of reality to be the total cause in bringing about the idea of God in his mind. Now, obviously, if the idea of God in Descartes' mind was a mere mode—and he being a thinking substance—on the basis of his own theory there can be no doubt that Descartes could have been the sole author of his idea of God. Descartes' claim that degrees of reality apply to objective existence as distinct from formal existence is the weakest link in his first argument for God's existence.

II *The Causal Principle*

Descartes' next step in his search for the existence of someone other than himself is to present the causal principle. One might, of course, also regard his introduction of the causal principle as the presentation of a new premise for the purpose of demonstrating God's existence. Commenting on the principle, he writes:

Now it is manifest by the natural light that there must at least be as much reality in the efficient and total cause as in its effect. For, pray, whence can the effect derive its reality, if not from the cause?

And in what way can this cause communicate this reality to it, unless it possessed it in itself? and from this it follows not only that something cannot proceed from nothing, but likewise that what is more perfect—that is to say, which has more reality within itself—cannot proceed from the less perfect.[14]

In this passage Descartes presents two statements of the principle of causality. They are:

    (1) "Something cannot proceed from nothing"; and
    (2) "There must at least be as much reality in the efficient and total cause as in its effect."

For Descartes, who at this point has liberated himself from his former prejudices, the second of these propositions is as self-evident as the first. This is apparent from the fact that he introduces (2) with the remark that it is to him "manifest by the natural light." But it may not be self-evident to his readers, who as yet may not have liberated themselves from their uncritical adherence to the senses. They no doubt are certain of the truth of (1), which is the famous maxim *ex nihilo, nihil fit* ("from nothing, nothing comes"); but Descartes fears that they may be uncertain about the truth of (2) and so he tries to demonstrate it. The argument consists in showing that a person cannot rationally accept (1) and deny (2); that, in fact, they are different formulations of the same causal principle. For suppose, he argues, that (2) was false and that what is less real can bring about what is more real, there would then be an increment of reality which came from nothing, but this is contrary to (1).

Descartes next contends that (2) applies to objective as well as formal reality: "And this [meaning the causal principle] is not only evidently true of those effects which possess actual or formal reality but also of the ideas in which we consider merely what is termed objective reality." True, says Descartes, "an idea has no formal reality other than what it acquires from the mind of which it is only a mode." "But," he continues, "in order that an idea should contain some one certain objective reality rather than another, it must without doubt derive it from some cause in which there is at least as much formal reality as this idea contains of objective reality."[15] It is apparent from this latter passage why Descartes believed that we can assign degrees to the objective reality of an idea as distinct from its formal reality. The reason is, declares Descartes, that there is a cause for the objective reality of an idea distinct from its existence as a mere mode of the mind:

Thus, if anyone has in his mind the idea of any machine showing high skill in its construction, it is certainly quite reasonable to ask what is the cause of that idea; and it is not sufficient to answer that the idea is nothing outside the mind, and hence can have no cause, but can merely be conceived; for here the whole question is—what is that which causes it to be conceived? Nor will it suffice to say that the mind itself is its cause, being the cause of its own acts; for this is not disputed, the question being the cause of the objective artifice which is in the idea.[16]

Descartes is right; we can and often do meaningfully ask for the cause of the objective existence of an idea as distinct from inquiring into its formal reality. Descartes can meaningfully ask how he acquired the idea of a perfect Being and that of an ingenious machine. But where I think Descartes is mistaken is in his inferring from this fact that God and the machine in his mind have degrees of reality distinct from their formal natures as modes of the mind. From a logical point of view, such an inference cannot be valid. To see that it is not, consider the following: I can ask why Jones is dancing; and, after receiving a satisfactory answer, I can further meaningfully ask, why is he dancing the waltz? But from this it surely does not follow that his dancing the waltz has in some sense or other a degree of reality distinct from the mere fact that he is dancing. Descartes may be right: the only plausible account for the fact that he has an idea of an absolutely perfect being in his mind is that God exists, but the causal explanation cannot be based on Descartes' claim that every idea in his mind has a cause which contains at least as much reality formally as the idea contains objectively.[17]

III *The Idea of God*

After presenting his causal principle and applying it to ideas as objectively existing in his mind, Descartes feels that he is

now in a position to establish whether or not there exists someone other than himself. He can accomplish this task by taking
an inventory of his ideas in order to see whether there is at least
one of them which he could not have brought about all by
himself:

But what am I to conclude from it all in the end? It is this, that
if the objective reality of any one of my ideas is of such a nature
as clearly to make me recognize that it is not in me either formally
or eminently, and that consequently I cannot myself be the cause
of it, it follows of necessity that I am not alone in the world, but
that there is another being which exists, or which is the cause of
this idea.[18]

By the expression "in me formally," Descartes means that
the properties which by representation exist in the idea are
actually present in him. For instance, thought and desire are
ideas which represent properties which he possesses as a thinking being. And by the term "eminently" Descartes means that,
while he does not possess the properties which the idea has
by representation, he possesses superior ones. For example, the
ideas of figure and extension are contained in him as a thinking
substance eminently in that while he does not possess these
properties formally, he nevertheless has properties superior to
them. Now, given Descartes' position that for each idea there
must be a cause which contains either formally or eminently
all the properties that are contained in the idea objectively,
it follows that, if Descartes has at least one idea which contains
one or more properties which is not contained in him, either
formally or eminently, then Descartes has the right to be certain
that he is not "alone in the world."

He first takes an inventory of his ideas: "But of my ideas,
beyond that which represents me to myself, as to which there
can here be no difficulty, there is another which represents a
God, and there are others representing corporeal and inanimate
things, others angels, others animals, and others again which
represent to me men similar to myself."[19] Descartes is certain
that he could have originated those ideas which represent men,
animals, and angels by combining aspects of the ideas of

corporeal things, himself, and God. For instance, the idea of an angel is that of a being who is greater than himself and far inferior to God; the idea of a man is a combination of an entity that thinks, which is derived from reflecting on his own mental activity, and a corporeal body. Descartes, consequently, has no unquestionable ground for believing that angels, men (remember Descartes as yet does not know that he is a man), and animals exist. While he cannot derive his ideas of corporeal beings and their modes as a result of combining other kinds of ideas, he is, however, quite certain that he could have originated them all by himself. True, he perceives "magnitude or extension in length, breadth, or depth" clearly and distinctly, but there is nothing in these ideas "so great or so excellent" that they might not have originated solely from himself. And, as for color, heat, sound, scent, and so on, they are perceived with "so much obscurity and confusion," declares Descartes, that the likelihood is that they represent nothing real and are merely the product of some defect in his nature:

Hence there remains only the idea of God, concerning which we must consider whether it is something which cannot have proceeded from me myself. By the name "God" I understand a substance that is infinite, [eternal, immutable], independent, all-knowing, all-powerful, and by which I myself and everything else, if anything else does exist, have been created. Now all these characteristics are such that the more diligently I attend to them, the less do they appear capable of proceeding from me alone; *hence, from what has been already said, we must conclude that God necessarily exists.*[20]

In this passage, Descartes concludes his argument for God's existence. The argument can be formulated in the form of a syllogism. With the expression "What has been already said," Descartes is referring to the principle of causality as it applies to ideas existing objectively in his mind. This principle can serve as the major premise of the syllogism. The argument is as follows:

(1) for each and every idea in my mind, there is a cause which contains formally or eminently all the properties that are contained in the idea objectively;

(2) the idea of an absolutely perfect being, that is, God, exists objectively in my mind;

(3) hence, God exists.

One would have expected that once Descartes concluded that God exists, he would have proceeded to consider other matters; but he did not. For, in presenting his argument for God's existence, he had assumed that the idea of God is neither a negative (not real) idea nor a materially false one. He now wants to show that he is justified in making this assumption. There is a difference between a negative idea and one that is materially false. A negative idea refers to the absence of something real. For instance, ignorance and darkness are negative ideas, for the one refers merely to the absence of knowledge and the other to the absence of light. A materially false idea, on the other hand, is an idea which is taken to represent something which it does not. In his *Conversation with Burman*, Descartes gives as his example of a materially false idea the ordinary man's idea of color as a quality of a body: ". . . if I said that whiteness is a quality, even if I did not refer this idea to anything outside me, even if I said or supposed that there was not a single white object, nonetheless I might make a mistake in abstract about whiteness itself and its nature or idea."[21] The experience of color is a sensation, according to Descartes; and when the ordinary man has the idea that color is a property of corporeal bodies, he has, modern philosophers would say, "committed a category mistake." He has confused an item which belongs to the category of mind, that is, a sensation, with what pertains to the category of body. Descartes called such confusions "materially false ideas." Notice that, while the negative idea of ignorance can apply to a man or an angel, a materially false idea can not possibly apply to anything.

Descartes first tries to show that the idea of God is a real idea and not a negative one:

Nor should I imagine that I do not perceive the infinite by a true [real] idea, but only by the negation of the finite, just as I perceive repose and darkness by the negation of movement and of light; for, on the contrary, I see that there is manifestly more reality in infinite substance than in finite, and therefore that in some way

I have in me the notion of the infinite earlier than the finite—to wit, the notion of God before that of myself. For how would it be possible that I should know that I doubt and desire, that is to say, that something is lacking to me, and that I am not quite perfect, unless I had within me some idea of a Being more perfect than myself, in comparison with which I should recognize the deficiencies of my nature?[22]

When Descartes, in the above passage, says "in some way I have in me the notion of the infinite earlier than the finite," he is not using "earlier" in the temporal sense. "Infinite" and "finite," like "rest" and "motion," are contrast terms, and a person could not have in his mind one of the concepts involved without the other. Thus, if I am to acquire the concept of the infinite, I must do so at the same time as the concept of the finite. When Descartes says that I must have "the notion of God before myself," he is referring to a relation between a standard and something which, though falling far short of the standard, is judged by it. The standard is the idea of God, and the entity judged by it is himself. This type of argument is to be found in Plato's *Phaedo* where Socrates argues that no person could possibly judge that two pieces of wood were more or less equal unless implicit in his mind was the idea of perfect equality. In an analogous sense, Descartes could not apply value concepts, that is, his having or lacking knowledge or virtue, unless implicit in his mind was the idea of an absolutely perfect being. The idea of God is *before* Descartes' idea of himself in the sense that he judges his deficiencies and accomplishments by an ideal standard set by the idea of God. Descartes' point is that far from the idea of God being a negative one, it is the most real of all ideas. "I see," says Descartes, "that there is manifestly more reality in infinite substance than in finite substance." And while, no doubt, Descartes' idea of himself as a substance that thinks is not negative, that of himself as a finite being is negative, for he can only conceive his finitude as the absence in him of the infinite perfection of God.

Descartes' next step is to contend that the idea of God is not materially false because it is clear and distinct:

And we cannot say that this idea of God is perhaps materially false and that consequently I can derive it from naught [i.e., that possibly it exists in me because I am imperfect] . . . for, on the contrary, as this idea is very clear and distinct and contains within it more objective reality than any other, there can be none which is of itself more true, nor any in which there can be less suspicion of falsehood.[23]

When Descartes says that his idea of God is clear and distinct, he means that his idea of God embodies a rule by which he is able to distinguish *clearly* what is to be attributed to God and what is not. The rule is that no properties are to be attributed to God which presuppose or involve a limitation in his being; all the others are to be attributed to Him. For instance, we cannot attribute to God a body, for then He could not act at all places at the same time. Again, we cannot attribute to God the virtue of courage; for in order to be courageous, He has to be able to confront obstacles for which fortitude is required, but then he could not be all-powerful. On the other hand, we have to attribute to God infinite power and omniscience, for these attributes neither presuppose nor involve any limitation in his being.

While Descartes insists that the idea of God is not materially false but clear and distinct, he admits, however, that he really does not comprehend God's nature: "And this [the idea of God being clear and distinct] does not cease to be true although I do not comprehend the infinite, or though in God there is an infinitude of things which I cannot comprehend, nor possibly even reach in any way by thought; for it is of the nature of the infinite that my nature, which is finite and limited, should not comprehend it. . . ."[24] On the basis of the above mentioned rule, Descartes knows what *clearly* belongs to God and what does not, but he cannot *comprehend* the attributes which he is certain belong to God. For instance, he knows that God is all-powerful and completely good, but he does not understand the manner in which these attributes exist in God; for, unlike in finite beings, power and goodness in God are not distinct but necessarily connected.[25]

IV *The Second Argument for God's Existence*

On Descartes' authority, the first and second arguments can be regarded as one argument. In a letter to Denis Mesland, he writes: "It does not make much difference whether my second proof, the one based on our existence is regarded as different from the first proof or merely an explanation of it."[26] I shall, however, consider them to be distinct arguments, because I believe they are logically independent. In the first Descartes argues that, since he has an idea of God, God exists; in the second, he argues that, since he exists, God exists.

Descartes begins the second argument with the question: from whom do I then derive my existence? There are four possible answers: from myself, or from my parents, or from some other source less perfect than God, or from God. This is an exhaustive list of possibilities,[27] and if Descartes can demonstrate that he could not have been derived from the first three sources, he will have, given the truth of the causal principle, proved God's existence. The term "derive my existence" is ambiguous. It could mean the causal agency that brought Descartes into existence, or the causal agency which sustains his existence. His parents were at least *part* of the cause in the former sense and the sun in the latter. He could not have been born without his parents but he can continue to live without them. And, while the sun was not directly involved in his birth, the existence of the sun is essential in his continuing to exist. Descartes could not mean the former, since he cannot be absolutely certain that he did not always exist. He was well aware that he was concerned with cause in the latter sense, for he says: "For all the course of my life may be divided into an infinite number of parts, none of which is in any way dependent on the other; and thus from the fact that I was in existence a short time ago it does not follow that I must be in existence now, unless some cause at this instant, so to speak, produces me anew, that is to say, conserves me."[28]

Descartes introduces a further premise which he considers to be self-evident and which is essential to his argument, namely, that the same amount of power is required to conserve someone in existence as to create him for the first time. This truth is evident, according to Descartes, once one realizes that, from the fact that a person exists at any one moment, it does not follow that he will exist at the next one. Thus, if a person is to enjoy continuity in existence, he must, so to speak, be created out of nothing from moment to moment: "It is as a matter of fact perfectly clear and evident to all those who consider with attention the nature of time, that, in order to be conserved in each moment in which it endures, a substance has need of the same power and action as would be necessary to produce and create it anew, supposing it did not yet exist..."[29]

The first of the four alternatives which Descartes considers but then rejects is that he is the author of his own being. In presenting his reason he appeals to the principle that a substance has greater reality than a mode, and that, consequently, it requires far greater power to bring about, whether in the manner of creation or conservation, a substance than a mode. Now, if Descartes had the power to conserve himself in existence, that is, to create himself from one moment to the next, then he could not possibly have any deficiencies in knowledge, goodness, or power. Why not? Because, if he had the power to create himself, given the fact that he is a substance, he would have been able to endow himself with all the perfections of God, which, though sublime, are nevertheless modes. He concludes, "But were I myself the author of my being, I should doubt nothing and I should desire nothing, and finally no perfection would be lacking to me; for I should have bestowed on myself every perfection of which I possessed any idea and should thus be a God."[30]

The next alternative is that Descartes' existence is being conserved by some being other than himself, his parents, or God. Descartes insists, however, that this being, whoever he may be, must like himself, be a thinking substance and have the idea of God in his mind; since, if he is the cause of his existence, he must have at least as much reality as he has. Descartes allows the possibility of this alternative but only on one condition, namely, that the being who is the cause of his existence is not self-creative, for if he were, then, like Descartes, he would have bestowed upon himself all the perfections of God. Descartes, conserver himself, thus requires a conserver. What about this latter entity? He cannot be self-existent, for then he would have bestowed upon himself all the perfections of God. And what about his conserver, again the same point? We must finally arrive at a being who in fact is self-existent and has all the perfections of God, namely, God.[31]

Descartes next considers two ways in which one might try to evade his conclusion. The first is that Descartes depends for his existence on some being A; A in turn on B; B on C; and so on into infinity. We do not stop as above with a self-existent being who is God; we simply never stop. We have here an endless hierarchy of existent beings, each contributing to the existence of the member below him. There is no upper limit to this hierarchy; only a lowest member. Descartes rejects this possibility: "...there can be no regression into infinity, since what is in question is not so much the cause which formerly created me, as that which conserves me at the present time."[32] Like St. Thomas, Descartes allows the possibility of an infinite causal chain of parents giving birth to children stretching without end infinitely in the past. But he rejects the possibility of an infinite regress of dependent causes. If A depends for his existence on B, B on C, and so on, there must be a first member upon whom all the members depend for their existence, but this member depends on no one. Again, one might try to evade the conclusion that it is God who conserves Descartes' existence by arguing that, while it is true that all the perfections of God are required to conserve him, they need not, however, belong to one individual. There may be a number of semidivine beings, each with an attribute of God, who together possess all His attributes, and are presently employed in the enterprise of conserving Descartes' existence. This relationship is impossible, says Descartes, since the unity of all of God's attributes is one of his major attributes: "On the contrary, the unity, the simplicity, or the inseparability of all things which are in God is one of the principal perfections which I conceive to be in Him."[33]

The remaining candidates for the ultimate source of Descartes' existence besides God are his parents. Descartes, of course, is uncertain that he has ever had parents; for, strictly speaking, at present Descartes does not know that anyone exists besides himself as a thinking being. He feels, however, that every possible cause of his existence must be considered. Nevertheless, it is surprising that he should have considered his parents as a separate category from other finite beings. In the first place, even in accordance with the vulgar (nonphilosophical) opinion, his parents are not essential for conserving his existence. Second, in accordance with common sense, his parents, while essential in bringing about his existence, are not self-existent beings but themselves depend on other agencies for conserving their existence. Moreover, the reasoning Descartes had already employed for rejecting the possibility that his existence depends on himself or other finite substances applies as well to his parents.

Descartes' reason for rejecting his parents as a possible source for his total existence is stated as follows: "... although all that I have ever been able to believe of them were true, that does not make it follow that it is they who conserve me, nor are they even the authors of my being in any sense, insofar as I am a thinking being; since what they did was merely to implant certain dispositions in that matter in which the self— i.e., the mind, which alone I at present identify with myself— is by me deemed to exist."[34] This is an unfortunate passage, for Descartes is here making an assumption that the body and mind are distinct substances and originate in different ways. No doubt this position is part of his philosophy; but at the present stage of his argument, he has no right to introduce it. Actually, Descartes has no need of this premise because the reason he had used previously for rejecting himself and other finite substances as the ultimate source of his conservation applies to his parents as well.

All other possible candidates having been eliminated as a source for his existence, God alone remains; and, given the truth of the principle that whatever exists has a cause, it follows, declares Descartes, that God exists: "... We must of necessity conclude from the fact alone that I exist, or that the idea of a being supremely perfect—that is of God—is in me, that the proof of God's existence is grounded on the highest evidence."[35]

This second argument for God's existence, while not as ingenious nor as original as the first argument, is nevertheless, in my opinion, a better argument. The first argument had a premise which is clearly false. I have in mind the premise that degrees of reality apply to the objective existence of an idea as distinct from its formal existence. The second argument has no premise which is clearly false. I do not wish to imply, however, that all the premises in the second argument are unquestionably true, as Descartes seemed to think, but only that none of them are conspicuously false.

CHAPTER 7

The Ontological Argument and the Eternal Truths

DESCARTES had still a third argument for God's existence which appears in the *Fifth Meditation* and not in the third with his first two arguments. The reason for his not presenting it in the third is that, unlike his first two arguments, this argument requires for its validity that the principle "what is clearly and distinctly perceived is true" serve as a premise. But, as indicated previously, the indubitability of this principle requires that a nondeceiving God exist. This third argument can, therefore, only appear after God's existence has been demonstrated and the principle accepted as true. Kant was later to call this argument "the Ontological Argument." Actually, as I shall try to show, Descartes had two ontological arguments. The first is found in both the *Discourse* and the *Meditations* and the second in his *Replies to Objections*. It appears that, in the course of defending the argument which he had presented in his two texts, he actually discarded it and developed a different one.

In the *Meditations*, as a prelude to the ontological argument, Descartes introduces his conception of a "true and immutable nature":

And what I find here to be most important is that I discover in myself an infinitude of ideas of certain things which cannot be esteemed as pure negations, although they may possibly have no existence outside of my thought, and which are not framed by me, although it is within my power either to think or not to think them, but which possess natures which are true and immutable. For example, when I imagine a triangle, although there may nowhere in the world be such a figure outside my thought, or ever have

140

been, there is nevertheless in this figure a certain determinate nature, form, or essence, which is immutable and eternal, which I have not invented, and which in no wise depends on my mind, as appears from the fact that diverse properties of that triangle can be demonstrated, viz. that its three angles are equal to two right angles, that the greatest side is subtended by the greatest angle, and the like, which now, whether I wish it or do not wish it, I recognize very clearly as pertaining to it, although I never thought of the matter at all when I imagined a triangle for the first time, and which therefore cannot be said to have been invented by me.[1]

The point Descartes is making is that the properties which are true of the nature of a triangle are necessarily connected. Thus, if it is true of a figure that it has three sides, then it is necessarily also true of it that it has three angles and that the sum of the three angles is equal to two right angles and so on. This is not true of those ideas constructed in the imagination, whether arbitrarily for the idea of a satyr or by coordinating the data of the senses for a swan. The idea of a swan consists of a white color, long neck, black legs, red beak, and so on; but these properties are not necessarily connected. I can clearly and distinctly perceive that an entity can have any one of these properties without necessarily possessing any of the others. Consequently, the idea of a swan does not contain a true and immutable nature.

In one of his replies to the first set of objections, Descartes clarifies this matter further. Ideas like that of a winged horse or an existent lion which the mind has constructed by a mental synthesis can, by "a clear and distinct mental operation," be analyzed into discrete and separate elements. Thus, I can think of someone with the properties of a horse but without wings; or I can think of nothing that exists with the properties of a lion. Consequently, the ideas in this case do not contain true and immutable natures. On the other hand, when I think of a triangle, I cannot deny that its three angles are equal to two right angles or that the greatest side is subtended by the greatest angle "... by any clear and distinct mental operation, i.e. when I myself rightly understand what I say."[2]

In the Ontological Argument, Descartes claims that the idea of God contains a true and immutable nature; and that existence cannot be separated from God's properties (omnipotence, omni-science, and so on) by a "clear and distinct mental operation." Thus, the existence of God, contends Descartes, can be demon-strated like any true proposition in mathematics. In the *Dis-course*, after examining the idea of a perfect being, he writes: "I found that in this case existence was implied in it in the same manner in which the equality of its three angles to two right angles is implied in the idea of a triangle..."[3] And in the *Fifth Meditation*, he writes: "It is certain that I no less find the idea of God, that is to say, the idea of a supremely perfect Being, in me, than that of any figure or number whatever it is; and I do not know any less clearly and distinctly that an [actual and] eternal existence pertains to this nature than I know that all that which I am able to demonstrate of some figure or number truly pertains to the nature of this figure or number...."[4]

Descartes realized that his argument is contrary to a general rule which to many people seems to be self-evident, namely, the distinction in all cases between essence and existence: that is, between what defines a thing from the fact that it exists. Descartes felt that he must, if his argument is to be accepted, do more than simply propose as a premise: "we clearly and distinctly understand that to exist belongs to His true and immutable nature." Consequently, Descartes clarifies his position in a further passage in the *Meditations*: "It is in truth necessary for me to assert that God exists after having presupposed that He possesses every sort of perfection, since existence is one of these...."[5] Descartes' argument can be stated in the following syllogism: (1) the idea of God is that of a Being who embodies all perfections; (2) existence is a perfec-tion; (3) hence, God exists.

Gassendi, in anticipating Kant, challenged premise (2) of Descartes' argument:

Existence is a perfection neither in God nor in anything else; it is rather that in the absence of which there is no perfection ... this must be so if, indeed, that which does not exist has neither per-fection nor imperfection, and that which exists and has various perfections, does not have its existence as a particular perfection and as one of the number of its perfections, but as that by means of which the thing itself equally with its perfections is in existence, and without which neither can it be said to possess perfections, nor can perfections be said to be possessed by it.[6]

Existence is not a perfection as is omnipotence or omniscience, says Gassendi, for what lacks omnipotence is an imperfect being; but what lacks existence is nothing at all. Gassendi is arguing that there is a difference between the manner in which a perfection or an imperfection is attributed to a subject and the way in which existence is. When I say, "Socrates is wise," I am presupposing that Socrates either exists now or at some time in the past; for, if no individual has ever existed who is or was Socrates, then I could not truly or falsely say of him that he is wise or foolish, rich or poor, a philosopher or a laborer. On the other hand, when I say, "Socrates exists," I am not presupposing that he exists but rather affirming it.

In his reply to Gassendi, Descartes makes two points. The first is that existence, like omnipotence and omniscience, is a predicate attributed to a subject. This reply fails to meet Gassendi's objection, for, no doubt, existence functions as a predicate; but the whole thrust of Gassendi's criticism is that the manner in which existence is predicated of a subject differs from the way perfections are attributed to a subject. Descartes' second point is that "necessary existence, in the case of God is also a true property in the strictest sense of the word . . ."[7] In this statement, perhaps without realizing it, Descartes adopted a different ontological argument from the one he had presented in the *Fifth Meditation*; he replaced the statement "existence is a perfection" with the statement "necessary existence is a perfection." It is not the absence of existence which would deny God's being perfect, says Descartes, but the contingency of His existence; that is, the fact that though He exists, He need not necessarily have existed. Again, it is not the fact of God's existence that is a perfection, but the fact that He could not possibly not exist. This argument is not exposed to Gassendi's criticism, for not only am I not a perfect being because I lack omnipotence, omniscience, and so on but also because I am a contingent being and not a necessary one.

The argument, however, is incomplete; Descartes has yet
to show that he clearly and distinctly perceives that necessary
existence applies to God, that is, that God's perfections preclude the possibility that He does not exist. I, for instance,
clearly and distinctly perceive that necessary nonexistence applies to a square-triangle, and I can show this by demonstrating
that the conjunction of the properties of a square and that
of a triangle involve a contradiction. What Descartes has to
show is that it is contradictory, or, in some other sense, impossible, to attribute Godlike perfections to someone and claim
that His existence is not necessary but contingent. In one of
his replies to the first set of objections, Descartes does complete
the argument:

But yet if we attentively consider whether existence is congruous
with a being of the highest perfection, and what sort of existence
is so, we shall be able clearly and distinctly to perceive in the first
place that possible existence is at least predicable of it, as it is of
all other things of which we have a distinct idea, even of those
things which are composed by a fiction of the mind. *Further, because
we cannot think of God's existence as being possible, without at the
same time, and by taking heed of His immeasurable power, acknowledging that He can exist by His own might, we hence conclude that
He really exists and has existed from all eternity; for the light of
nature makes it most plain that what can exist by its own power
always exists.* And thus we shall understand that necessary existence
is comprised in the idea of a being of the highest power, not by any
intellectual fiction, but because it belongs to the true and immutable
nature of that being to exist.[8]

In discussing Descartes' second argument for God's existence
we noted that God is the cause of His own existence by the
mere fact that He possesses infinite power. Descartes now uses
this conception of God as the ground for inferring that it is
impossible that God not exist. The key expression in the above
passage is "... and by taking heed of His immeasurable power,
acknowledging that He can exist by His own might, we hence
conclude that He really exists." This inference is invalid. Descartes does not clearly distinguish the eternity of God from
the logical necessity of His existence. The fact that God "can

exist by His own might" at best indicates that He could not possibly have come into existence nor pass out of existence; and that, consequently, if He exists at any one time, then He necessarily exists at all other times. But the fact that God has the power to sustain his own existence in no way entails that He could not conceivably not exist. For it is perfectly consistent with God's nonexistence that *if* He existed, He would have infinite power and thus would be the cause of His eternal existence.

Both ontological arguments are, in my opinion, unacceptable, but for different reasons. The first, while valid in that the conclusion follows from the premises, contains, however, a false premise, that is, existence is a perfection. On the other hand, none of the premises in the second argument is clearly false; unfortunately, the conclusion does not follow from the premises. At best, this argument establishes that if an omnipotent being exists, then he is necessarily eternal; but it does not show that either an omnipotent being or an eternal being exists.

I   *The Creation of the Eternal Truths*

In 1630, Descartes wrote a letter to Mersenne in which he stated a doctrine which was to shock his contemporaries. While this doctrine does not appear in the *Discourse*, the *Meditations* or the *Principles*, it was not, however, a passing whim of his, for it recurs in a number of his letters and is to be found in two of his replies to objections. It was so unorthodox and so contrary to the prevailing theological opinion that Descartes was reluctant to make it public. The doctrine is that God is the creator of the eternal truths.

Descartes' contemporaries did not believe that the eternal truths were independent of God. To quote St. Thomas, "...we cannot say that the divine ideas are outside of God."[9] The eternal truths, or "the eternal essences," as they were sometimes called, were considered ideas in the intellect of God; consequently God's knowledge of them was not knowledge of a subject matter alien to His being but of his own mind. According to the prevalent orthodox opinion, however, the eternal truths were not created by God, for they are independent of His divine will.

In his letter to Mersenne, Descartes introduces his doctrine in the following words: "*You ask* me by *what kind of causality God established the eternal truths.* I reply: by the same kind as he created all things, that is to say, as their *efficient and total cause* . . . you ask also what necessitated God to create these truths; and I reply that just as He was free not to create the world so He was no less free to make it untrue that all the lines drawn from the centre of the circle to its circumference are equal . . . you ask what God did in order to produce them. I reply that *from all eternity he willed and understood them to be, and by that very fact he created them.*"[10] Descartes adds, however, that, while he knows this relationship to be true, he cannot really conceive or comprehend it. Thus, in a letter to Arnauld, he says: "But I do not think that we should ever say of anything that it cannot be brought about by God. For since everything involved in truth and goodness depends on His omnipotence, I would not dare to say that God cannot make a mountain without a valley, or that one and two should not be three. I merely say that He has given me such a mind that I cannot conceive a mountain without a valley, or an aggregate of one and two which is not three, and that such things involve a contradiction in my conception."[11]

Descartes gives his reason for adopting this position in one of his replies to the sixth set of objections. He says that it would be a contradiction to contend on the one hand that God is omnipotent and on the other that His freedom of action is limited by a standard of right and wrong or truth and error. For, were the latter the case, then there would be certain things which God could not possibly bring about; hence, He would not be omnipotent. God must have what Descartes calls "freedom of indifference," namely, there is no reason which determines or sways His will to act in one way rather than another: "For it is self-contradictory that the will of God should not have been from eternity indifferent to all that has come to pass or that ever will occur . . ."[12]

Descartes' doctrine seems, however, to be inconsistent with his general philosophical position. In the first place, there is no longer a clear distinction between necessary truths which could not possibly have been otherwise, such as "figure is a mode of an extended body," and universally true contingent propositions which could possibly have been false, such as "all men die." For, according to Descartes, both classes of propositions might have been false, for God could have created figure without extension as well as immortal men. True, in a letter to Mesland, he says that God willed the eternal truths to be necessary; since His nature is immutable His will must be so as well.[13] But what could God possibly do to make the distinction between that which is necessarily true from that which is unchangeably but contingently true? Does He, so to speak, say in His mind: "Let it be a necessary truth that 'figure is a mode of an extended body' and a contingent truth that 'all men die.'" The Divine words differ in the two cases, but how can we have here two different concepts, when the truth of both propositions is due either directly or indirectly to the agency of His will. Second, among the truths which God might have created otherwise are those involving conduct, such as "inflicting unnecessary pain is wicked," "justice is a virtue," "deception is wrong," and so on. But it would then seem to follow that in demonstrating the existence of a perfect Being, Descartes did not necessarily establish the existence of a God who is not a deceiver. For God might have willed that deception is a good without this fact in any way impairing His perfection.

There are passages, however, in his letters where Descartes makes statements which seem outrightly to contradict the notion of God as the creator of the eternal truths, or at least to qualify it significantly. In a letter to Henry More, as late as 1649, Descartes says that, if something is possible, like dividing an atom, then it is a contradiction to say that God is all-powerful but cannot divide it; but where something is impossible, such as, what has been done can be undone, it is no contradiction to say that God cannot bring it about. Why not? Because, as he says: "we perceive it to be altogether impossible, and so it is no defect of power in God not to do it."[14] In this letter, Descartes, contrary to his stated doctrine above, is adopting Aquinas' position: "...nothing that implies a contradiction falls under the scope of God's omnipotence."[15] And, even in those letters where Descartes states his doctrine, he somewhat qualifies it. God, says Descartes, being simple in the sense that there are no diverse attributes in Him, there can be no distinction between His will and His intellect. We could just as well say that the eternal truths constitute God's understanding as to say they are products of His will. Thus, Descartes writes to Mersenne: "In God it is only one thing to will and to know . . . from the very fact that He wishes anything, He therefore knows it; and, therefore, only is such a thing true."[16] And to Mesland he writes: "We should not conceive any preference or priority between the intellect and the will."[17]

But in that case God could not, contrary to some of his statements, bring about that two and three make more or less than five or that injustice is a virtue. For the eternal truths constitute His understanding as well as being products of His will. According to this position, God does not consult His understanding for the knowledge that two and two make four as the Thomists claim. Nor does He proclaim the truth of this proposition by an arbitrary act of will as Descartes sometimes seems to say. Rather His knowledge of the truth of the proposition and His proclamation of its truth constitute an identical eternal occurrence.

Which of the two positions was Descartes': the first, in which God could have brought about logical and moral impossibilities, or the second, which I have just outlined above? I really do not know, but because of my respect for Descartes' good sense, I suspect that it was the second.

CHAPTER 8

Descartes' Proof of the External World

DESCARTES believes that he has now established the in-dubitable fact that the ultimate source of his existence is God and that, consequently, he is now in the position to discard the demon hypothesis and to rely on his faculties for the acquisition of knowledge. He presently knows of the existence of only two beings: himself as a thinking being and God. He would like to proceed to prove the existence of the world, that is, the existence of bodies and other finite minds. But he now finds an obstacle to his journey of discovery. There are two facts which are certainly true and yet appear to be incompatible, namely, that he was created by a nondeceiving God and that he occasionally makes false judgments. Descartes feels that, if he is going to rely unconditionally on his cognitive powers, he must discover the source of his errors and absolve God of responsibility for them.

Descartes addresses himself to this problem by first distinguishing the understanding (perception) from the will. In the *Principles*, he refers to them as the "general modes of the mind": "Thus sense perception, imagining, and conceiving things that are purely intelligible, are just different methods of perceiving; but desiring, holding in aversion, affirming, denying, doubting, all these are the different modes of willing!"[1] The understanding and the will, as this passage from the *Principles* indicates, constitute a complete characterization of the activities of the mind.

In the context of his problem, Descartes says two things about the understanding. First, the perceptions of the understanding are, *strictly speaking*, neither true nor false. This fact applies not only to the sense perception of a visual image but to a clear and distinct idea as well. The understanding

149

provides the material upon which true and false judgments
are made, and judgments, as the above passage indicates, are
a mode of the will. Second, there is no defect in the understanding from which error can arise. True, the understanding is
limited: "There is possibly an infinitude of things in the world
of which I have no idea in my understanding." But, then, adds
Descartes, I am a limited being; and "... there is no reason to
prove that God should have given me a greater faculty of
knowledge than He has given me ..."[2] Descartes is here distinguishing ignorance from error. Ignorance is simply the absence
of knowledge, but error involves false judgment as well. For
instance, I am ignorant of higher mathematics; but, unlike most
mathematicians, I have never committed an error in this subject, for the simple reason that I have never ventured to make
judgments about it. There is no difficulty in accounting for the
fact that God created ignorant persons. There can only exist
one infinite being; consequently, in creating persons, God can
only create finite ones, who, not being omniscient, necessarily
have to be ignorant of certain things. There is, however, says
Descartes, a serious problem as to why a nondeceiving God
created persons who make false judgments, for clearly he could
have created persons who never commit errors.

According to Descartes, the will, unlike the understanding, is
"perfect" and "not subject to limits." And, more than any
other aspect of his nature, it is freedom of will which con-
vinces Descartes that he bears "the image of similitude of God":

For although the power of will is incomparably greater in God than
in me, both by reason of the knowledge and the power which, conjoined with it, render it stronger and more efficacious, and by reason
of its object, inasmuch as in God it extends to a great many things;
it nevertheless does not seem to me greater if I consider it formally
and precisely in itself: for the faculty of will consists alone in our
having the power of choosing to do a thing or choosing not to do it
(that is, to affirm or deny, to pursue or to shun it), or rather it
consists alone in the fact that in order to affirm or deny, pursue or
shun those things placed before us by the understanding, *we act so
that we are unconscious that any outside force constrains us in doing
so.* For in order that I should be free it is not necessary that I
should be indifferent as to the choice of one or the other of two

contraries; but contrariwise the more I lean to the one—whether I recognise clearly that the reasons of the good and true are to be found in it, or whether God so disposes my inward thought—the more freely do I choose and embrace it. . . . Hence this indifference which I feel, when I am not swayed to one side rather than to the other by lack of reason, is *the lowest grade of liberty,* and rather evinces a lack or negation in knowledge than a perfection of will. . . .[3]

Descartes' characterization of freedom of choice—that "we act so that we are unconscious that any outside force constrains us in doing so"—seems to me to be inadequate. There are, I believe, a number of different types of actions, not freely chosen, which are not eliminated by Descartes' characterization from the set of freely chosen actions. If a thief holds me up I am free to choose, according to this position, to safeguard my valuables because I am unconscious of any outside force which keeps me from resisting him. Again, contrary to Descartes, I might truly say of a kleptomaniac that he was not free to steal so and so, despite the fact that he was not conscious of an outside force which compelled him to steal. And, again, consider a person who, under hypnosis, is told to perform a certain action which he subsequently performs when awake. He is under the impression that he is freely choosing to perform the action; but we, unlike Descartes, knowing the ultimate cause of his action would surely hesitate to say that he was acting freely.

Descartes, however, seems to be right in his contention that a person who performs the right thing because he knows that there are good reasons for his doing so is acting freely. For instance, I have good reasons for keeping my foot on the brake when a pedestrian crosses the street; it would, however, be absurd to conclude that I was not acting freely because I could not choose to place my foot on the accelerator. There is, however, an exception to Descartes' claim. What I have in mind is the person who does the right thing because he is obligated to do it, though he would much prefer not to. We consider such a person not to have acted freely; for he was morally constrained to do his duty and, therefore, could not freely choose to do what he would have liked to. Nevertheless, he acted for the best of reasons. Descartes is also right when he claims that freedom of indifference *in his case* is "The lowest grade of liberty." (God's freedom of indifference, as was indicated in the last chapter, was held by Descartes to be entailed by His omnipotence.) To appreciate Descartes' point, consider A and B: both choose to perform action p, but A has a reason for his choice while B does not. Now, in one sense, they are both free, because neither is constrained by an external force from choosing any of the available options. But A's freedom is superior to B's, because he is not constrained from choosing what he knows to be a good reason for his preference; whereas B's freedom is of less value to him because, while he is not constrained from choosing p, he knows of no reason why he should do so. And, aside from the intrinsic value of being in a position to make a free choice, his freedom is of little use to him.

From the above reflections, Descartes concludes that error is neither due to his will nor to his understanding. How, then, is error possible? Descartes gives his answer in the following passage:

From all this I recognise that the power of will which I have received from God is not of itself the source of my errors—for it is very ample and very perfect of its kind—any more than is the power of understanding; for since I understand nothing but by the power which God has given me for understanding, there is no doubt that all that I understood, I understand as I ought, and it is not possible that I err in this. Whence then, come my errors? They come from the sole fact that since the will is much wider in its range and compass than the understanding, I do not restrain it within the same bounds, but extend it also to things which I do not understand; and as the will is of itself indifferent to these, it easily falls into error and sin, and chooses the evil for the good, or the false for the true.[4]

Error, according to Descartes, is due to the fact that, being finite, his understanding is limited and, consequently, there are many things which he does not perceive clearly and distinctly; but, being made in the image of God, his will is unlimited, and he is thus able to judge as true things which he does not clearly and distinctly perceive. True, he might have, if he were exercising his freedom properly, confined himself to judging as true only what he clearly understands to be true; but, since his will is unlimited, he need not do so. Error, like evil, turns out for Descartes to be a misuse of free will, "for the light of nature teaches us that knowledge of the understanding should always precede the determinations of the will."[5] Descartes has as yet not discovered that he is a man whose concerns are not merely theoretical but practical as well. When he does make this discovery, the above teaching from "the light of nature" will have to be qualified.

Having discovered the source of error, Descartes absolves God of any responsibility for its occurrence:

For in fact it is not an imperfection in God that He has given me the liberty to give or withhold my assent from certain things as to which He has not placed a clear and distinct knowledge in my understanding; but it is without doubt an imperfection in me not to make a good use of my freedom, and to give my judgement readily on matters which I only understand obscurely.[6]

This conclusion eliminates the last obstacle to Descartes' right to employ all his faculties for the purpose of acquiring knowledge; for not only had he demonstrated that the source of his existence is a nondeceiving God, but he had also explained why this fact is not inconsistent with his committing errors. Descartes is now prepared to try to establish the existence of the physical world and dispel the last remnant of his state of skepticism.

I *The Argument from the Imagination*

Descartes' first argument for the existence of bodies begins with the premise that bodies may possibly exist insofar as they possess the properties of the objects of pure mathematics:

Nothing further now remains but to inquire whether material things exist. And certainly I at least know that these may exist insofar as they are considered as the objects of pure mathematics, since in this aspect I perceive them clearly and distinctly. For there is no doubt that God possesses the power to produce everything that I am capable of perceiving with distinctness, and I have never deemed that anything was impossible for Him, unless I found a contradiction in attempting to conceive it clearly.[7]

Descartes is not claiming that corporeal bodies can only have the properties of purely mathematical objects. He is not, for instance, denying the possibility that bodies may be colored. His point is rather that, if there are material bodies, the only thing he can be certain about them is that they have properties such as figure and size, which are studied in pure mathematics, because he clearly and distinctly perceives that the objects of pure mathematics do not involve a contradiction. Since he cannot be sure that this is the case with regard to non-mathematical conceptions of material bodies, he will confine himself to establishing that there exists bodies with mathematical properties and leave open the issue as to whether they have other kinds of properties.

The second step in his argument is to distinguish the imagination from conception or what he sometimes calls "pure intellection." "For example, when I imagine a triangle," says Descartes, "I do not conceive it only as a figure comprehended by three lines, but I also apprehend these three lines as present by the power and inward vision of my mind. . . ." To develop the difference between imagination and pure intellection, Descartes makes two further points. First, there are many things which we can conceive but cannot imagine. I can conceive a chiliagon, that is, a figure with a thousand sides, with the same ease as I conceive a triangle, but while I can form an image of a triangle, I cannot form one of a chiliagon.[8] In his replies to the objections of Hobbes and Gassendi, Descartes cites God and the self as a thinking substance as examples of things which he can conceive but cannot imagine. There is, however, a difference between the latter two and a chiliagon. An ideal imaginer who can form an image of whatever could conceivably be imagined can form one of a chiliagon or a myriagon but not of the self or God. It appears that the scope of what is imaginable is confined to what could possibly be perceived by the senses. A chiliagon or a myriagon are possible objects of sense perception; God and the self are not. Second, there is an effort of will required in order to imagine something. This is not true of conception. For instance, when I form an image of a pentagon, that is, a five-sided figure, I have to attend to each of its sides to make sure that they are no more or less than five: "And, thus, I clearly recognize that I have need of a particular effort of mind in order to effect the act of imagination, such as I do not require in order to understand, and this particular effort of mind clearly manifests the difference which exists between imagination and pure intellection."[9]

In the following passage, Descartes introduces his third step in the argument and draws his conclusion:

> I remark besides that this power of imagination which is in one, inasmuch as it differs from the power of understanding, is in no wise a necessary element in my nature, or in [my essence, that is to say, in] the essence of my mind; for, although I did not possess it I should doubtless ever remain the same as I now am, from which it appears that we might conclude that it depends on something which differs from me. And I easily conceive that if some body exists with which my mind is conjoined and united in such a way that it can apply itself to consider it when it pleases, it may be that by this means it can imagine corporeal objects; so that this mode of thinking differs from pure intellection only inasmuch as mind in its intellectual activity in some manner turns on itself, and considers some of the ideas which it possesses in itself; while, in imagining it turns towards the body and there beholds in it something conformable to the idea which it has either conceived of itself or perceived by the senses.[10]

The first thing to note in this passage is that the expression, "I remark that this power of imagination . . . is in no wise a necessary element in my nature," is ambiguous. It could mean either of the following: (1) the power of imagination is not essential for my existence as a finite mind; (2) some individual could possibly be Descartes, even if he lacked the power of imagination. That these two propositions are not identical in meaning is apparent when one considers that Descartes has a finite mind, and no doubt Eskimo have finite minds, and persons were born in the first century with finite minds; but it would be absurd to claim that Descartes could have been the same individual if he were born an Eskimo or in the first century B.C. There are certain properties which are essential if someone is to possess a finite mind and others which are essential in his being the person that he is. Now, it is obvious that Descartes could only have meant (1); for at this stage of his inquiry, he as yet does not know that he is a man, let alone a Frenchman living in the seventeenth century. The only thing about himself that he has a right to be certain of is that he is a finite thinking substance who is conserved by the agency of God in existence.

Second, Descartes is able to maintain that a finite mind can exist without the power of imagination, because he believes that there are two kinds of memory, namely, spiritual as well as corporeal memory. In the latter case, a memory state necessarily involves the presence of an image; this is not so in the former case. To Mersenne, Descartes writes: "Moreover, in addition to the bodily memory, whose impressions can be explained by these folds in the brain, I believe that there is also in our intellect another sort of memory, which is altogether spiritual, and is not found in animals."[11]

Third, it is apparent that Descartes' conclusion that images are corporeal in nature and involve the presence of a body is not deduced from the premises but is rather presented as an explanatory hypothesis. There are two reasons why he did not present his argument in a deductive form. For one thing, from the fact that the power of the imagination is not essential to Descartes' existence as a finite mind, it does not follow that the imagination partly depends on something extrinsic to his mind. Moreover, even if the latter were true, it does not follow that this other thing resembles his images and, consequently, is a body. Descartes realizes that he can only propose his conclusion as a hypothesis; but, as he notes, a hypothesis, no matter how adequate, can never provide certainty but, at best, only a high degree of probability: "I easily understand, I say, that the imagination could be thus constituted if it is true that body exists; and because I can discover no other convenient mode of explaining it, I conjecture with probability that body does exist. . . ."[12] The argument from imagination, while it is a good one, does not serve Descartes' purpose, for what he seeks is not a conclusion which is highly probable but one that is certain. Probable conclusions, as he had indicated at the very start of his inquiry, can never provide the necessary foundations for the sciences.

II *The Argument from Sense Perception*

The second argument for the existence of the physical world appears in the *Sixth Meditation* after a lengthy presentation of both the beliefs he had held when he was philosophically unsophisticated and the reasons (such as the occurrence of dreams) which, in the *First Meditation*, led him to adopt a skeptical position toward the existence of bodies. He writes: "But now that I begin to know myself better, and to discover more clearly the author of my being, I do not in truth think that I should rashly admit all the matters which the senses seem to teach us, but, on the other hand, I do not think that I should doubt them all universally."[13] In the *Sixth Meditation*, Descartes is in a different cognitive situation than he was in the first; now he is certain of two things which he did not know then, namely, that he is a thinking substance and that a nondeceiving God exists. Descartes then notes that present in himself are the faculties of imagination and sensation which he is certain are not essential for his existence. He notes also that he appears to change his position from one place to another as to assume different figures, which, if these things are real, belong to him as an extended substance distinct from his existence as a spiritual one. The above remarks prepare the setting for his presentation of the second argument.

In the first argument, Descartes concerned himself with the faculty of imagination; in the present argument, he considers sense perception. These two faculties differ in a significant respect. The imagination is both an active and a passive faculty, because the mind not only contemplates an image but is actively involved in producing it. For example, I might exert myself in trying to imagine an old friend's face. The image, however, is not presented to me from an outside source; on the contrary, it appears to form itself before my mind as the result of my mental exertion. The faculty of imagination is, so to speak, both the producer of images and the audience which contemplates them. Not so the faculty of sense perception. Descartes considers it to be only a passive faculty, because it can only receive and recognize sensory objects but can play no active role in producing them. I can, with my eyes and ears set myself to have a sense experience; but, unless some object (whether a figure or a color) were presented before my mind from some source other than my faculty of sense perception, the senses would be of no use to me. Now, since sense objects are not produced by the faculty of sense perception, declares Descartes, there must be some active faculty, whether in me as a thinking substance or in some substance other than myself, which is the source of these ideas: "There is certainly further in me a certain passive faculty of perception, that is, of receiving and recognising the ideas of sensible things, but this would be useless to me [and I could in no way avail myself of it], if there were not either in me or in some other thing another active faculty capable of forming and producing these ideas."[14]

The next step in Descartes' argument is to show that the active faculty does not belong to him as a substance whose nature is to think:

But this active faculty cannot exist in me [inasmuch as I am a thing that thinks], seeing that it does not presuppose thought, and also that those ideas are often produced in me without my contributing in any way to the same, and often even against my will; it is thus necessarily the case that the faculty resides in some substance different from me in which all the reality which is objectively in the ideas that are produced by this faculty is formally or eminently contained, as I remarked before.[15]

It is not apparent what Descartes' first reason is for denying that the active faculty does not reside in himself insofar as he is a thinking substance. What does he mean by the expression "seeing that it does not presuppose thought," which is a premise he uses to draw his conclusion? He could have meant two different things: first, that the corporeal images which he perceived with his senses, unlike concepts, judgments, passions, and even sensations, could conceivably exist without being (with the exception of God) perceived by a mind; and second, that properties such as figure and magnitude which he perceives to belong to the corporeal images necessarily could not be formally properties of thinking unextended substances. There is no ground in the text or elsewhere for choosing between these two interpretations. Descartes' second reason presents no difficulties of interpretation. Already, in the *Third Meditation,* he had mentioned that his sense objects are not the products of his will and that sometimes they present themselves before his mind against his wishes. Notice that Descartes did not consider the possibility that he was willfully producing the sense objects without his being aware of this fact. He considered it to be self-evident that, if a person knows that something is occurring and if he is the agent who is willfully and *directly* bringing it about, then he cannot fail to be aware that he is bringing it about. This principle was implicit in the *Cogito* argument; for Descartes was not merely conscious that there was an instance of doubt occurring but also that he was the agent who was actively doubting. To be sure, according to Descartes, a person can doubt that he is moving his arm when his movement is an intentional act. But this doubt is possible because he doubts that he has an arm. What he cannot doubt is that he is bringing about what appears to be a movement of his arm.

Descartes' two reasons for concluding that the active faculty for his sense objects does not reside in himself, at best, in accordance with his own standard of knowledge, provides probability but not certainty. Previously, Descartes had stated that he as a thing that thinks might possibly have a hidden faculty which he is not aware of in himself, and which is not a mode of his will, but produces his sense objects, including his corporeal images. Descartes' reasons do not indubitably eliminate this possibility but merely indicate its unlikelihood. In the *Third Meditation,* Descartes had considered the second of the reasons as possible grounds for claiming that his adventitious ideas came from an external source but dismissed it as insufficient to provide certainty for the conclusion. Considering that at this point in his argument he has as yet made no appeal to God's veracity, I see no reason why he should have dismissed the reason in the *Third Meditation* and accepted it in the sixth.

Having rejected his mind as the causal agency that produces the objects of sense perception, Descartes considers three other alternatives: "And this substance is either a body, that is, a corporeal nature in which there is contained formally [and really] all that which is objectively [and by representation] in those

ideas, or it is God Himself, or some other creature more noble
than body in which that same is contained eminently."[16] The
three alternatives together with himself as a thinking substance
constitute an exhaustive set of possibilities. Consequently, if
Descartes can eliminate all alternatives except a body as possible
causal accounts, he will have demonstrated the existence of the
physical world. Notice that this argument has the same formal
structure as the second argument for God's existence. In both
arguments, some fact is presented for which a causal account
has to be found. In Descartes' second argument for God's
existence, the fact was the continuity of his existence from
moment to moment and in the present argument it is the fact
that there are sense objects present to his understanding. Now,
if such an argument is to establish a certain truth and not
merely a probable one, then two conditions must be fulfilled.
The alternatives considered must exhaust all possible causal
explanations, and those rejected must be shown to be inconceivable as causal accounts. No doubt Descartes' argument
satisfied the first condition; what is at issue is whether it satisfied the second. Another point of importance is that the phrase
"some other creature more noble than body" may refer to
himself as a mind as well as to any other finite substance. Thus,
if Descartes can demonstrate that neither God nor a creature
more noble than body contains the active faculty, he will
have proved the existence of physical bodies, notwithstanding
the fact that in this part of the argument he does not mention
himself as a thinking substance—a possible cause of his sense
objects.

In order to eliminate the possibility that God or some other
creature more noble than body contains the active faculty,
Descartes appeals to two indubitable facts. The first is that
he has a "very great inclination" to believe that his sense
objects are caused by material bodies; the second is that the
ultimate source of his existence is a God who would not deceive
him: "But, since God is no deceiver, it is very manifest that
He does not communicate to me these ideas immediately and
by Himself, nor yet by the intervention of some creature in
which their reality is not formally, but only eminently, contained. For, since He has given me no faculty to recognize

that this is the case, but, on the other hand, a very great in-clination to believe [that they are sent to me or] that they are conveyed to me by corporeal objects, I do not see how He could be defended from the accusation of deceit if these ideas were produced by causes other than corporeal objects. Hence, we must allow that corporeal things exist."[17]

The phrase "a very strong inclination to believe" is misleading with regard to what Descartes wishes to convey, for a person may have a very strong inclination to believe that the earth is flat or that all Frenchmen are charming. The inclinations in these cases are the result of a person's education, cultural back-ground, and the very many circumstances that contribute to his tendency to adopt one set of beliefs rather than another. What is especially important in Descartes' argument is that the belief that physical bodies exist is "a natural belief," that is, one that is "taught to him by nature." Consequently, in order to understand this argument, a few comments are in order about Descartes' doctrine of natural beliefs.

III *Natural Beliefs*

The doctrine of natural beliefs first appears when Descartes considers those beliefs which he held before he adopted a skeptical attitude toward the existence of the world:

But when I inquired, why, from some, I know not what, painful sensation, there follows sadness of mind, and from the pleasurable sensation there arises joy, or why this mysterious pinching of the stomach which I call hunger causes me to desire to eat, and dryness of throat causes a desire to drink, and so on, I could give no reason excepting that nature taught me so . . .[18]

Subsequently, Descartes mentions three other things which are taught to him by nature. First, that he has a body and that there are numerous other bodies which surround his own, some of which are to be sought after and others avoided. Second, that it is from his own and other bodies that the objects of his sense perception proceed. And third, that corresponding to the different sorts of colors, sounds, scents, and so on there are in the bodies from which these sense perceptions proceed certain variations which correspond to them and which, Descartes cautiously adds, need not resemble them.[19]

But there are, adds Descartes, certain beliefs which nature *appears* to have taught him but which he had never received from her. Instead, they were brought about by his habit of forming "inconsiderate judgements on things." Descartes gives three illustrations of pseudonatural beliefs: empty space exists; bodies have the properties of heat, color, taste, and so on exactly as we experience them; stars and distant towers have the sizes they appear to have when seen from a distance.[20]

Natural beliefs have the following characteristics. First, they are not acquired as a result of circumstances and learning but are instinctive beliefs which are as much part of our natural inheritance as humans as is the fact that we are born with brains and hearts. Second, no person, even an extreme skeptic, can fail to accept these beliefs for the practical activities of life, for they are indispensable for the purposes of survival and well-being. Third, while these beliefs are not indubitable as are the eternal truths, which the *light* of nature teaches us, nevertheless it requires a very great effort of will to sustain an attitude of doubt toward them.

In a remarkable passage, Descartes distinguishes the teachings of nature from those of the light of nature and relates them both to God:

But in order that in this there should be nothing which I do not conceive distinctly, I should define exactly what I really understand when I say that I am taught somewhat by nature. For here I take nature in a more limited signification than when I term it the sum of all the things given me by God, since in this sum many things are comprehended which only pertain to mind (and to these I do not refer in speaking of nature) such as the notion which I have of the fact that what has once been done cannot ever be undone and an infinitude of such things which I know by the light of nature [without the help of the body]; . . . for in talking of nature I only treat of those things given by God to me as a being composed of mind and body.[21]

I would take issue with Descartes' contention that all natural beliefs are true. It seems to me that the conviction that people have that their sensations are spatially located in their bodies qualifies as a natural belief despite the fact that, according to Descartes' philosophical position, this belief is false. There are two facts about this belief which one should bear in mind. First, the belief is extremely useful to the survival and well-being of man. For instance, because it seems to me that there is an intense pain located on the surface of my left arm I can immediately locate the area of bodily damage and take the appropriate steps to eliminate it. Second, as a result of employing my faculty of reason I can clearly and distinctly perceive that sensations, being modes of the mind, cannot be located in my body. Consequently, considering these two facts, I cannot accuse God of deceiving me by programming me as a body-mind complex with this illusion; for on the one hand the illusion is essential for my survival, and on the other hand he has given me a faculty by which I can liberate myself from it. Toward the end of the *Sixth Meditation* Descartes implies the very things which I have just stated.[22]

Let us now apply Descartes' doctrine of natural beliefs to his second argument for the existence of material bodies. Obviously, he cannot utilize the full doctrine. He does not, for instance, know that he is a body-mind complex or that all people at all times with the exception of a few philosophers accept these natural beliefs, since he does not as yet know that there exist finite minds besides himself. He knows, however, that he cannot dispense with these beliefs in the conduct of his life; further, he knows that they are, so to speak, native to his nature, since he requires a great effort of will to adopt and sustain a skeptical attitude toward them.

Now, since God is no deceiver, Descartes reasons that He would not have created him with natural instincts which lead him to adopt false beliefs unless He had endowed him with the means of detecting their falsehood. Consequently, Descartes adopted a principle which states that if a natural belief is clearly and distinctly perceived to be possibly true, then it is necessarily true. This principle is itself clearly and distinctly perceived. It is not, however, an immediate intuition but requires the premise that whatever exists is created by a benevolent nondeceiving God. A word of caution, the term "neces-

sarily" in the principle does not signify that certain natural
beliefs are necessary truths. A natural belief is "taught by
nature" and not like a necessary truth by "the light of nature."
To put this matter in a more modern idiom, the instinctive
acceptance of natural beliefs is part of the programming which
God has bestowed on man as a body-mind complex, whereas
the ability to intuit necessary truths is part of the programming
of the self as a thinking substance. The term "necessarily" in
the above principle indicates that it cannot be the case that a
natural belief is *possibly* true but is false. In the same sense
one would say that if Jones is a grandparent, then necessarily
he had a child. Obviously, Jones' having a child is not a necessary truth; it cannot be the case, however, that Jones is a
grandparent and has not had a child.

Descartes' argument for the existence of the physical world
can be formulated as follows:

(1) if a natural belief is clearly and distinctly perceived to
be possibly true, then it is necessarily true;
(2) it is a natural belief that the objects of sense perception
proceed from material bodies;
(3) I clearly and distinctly perceive that bodies possessing
mathematical properties can possibly exist;
(4) hence, it is certain that bodies possessing mathematical
properties exist.

IV *Dreaming and Waking*

Descartes now knows that the physical world exists, but he
may not be able to utilize this principle as a foundation principle
for the sciences, because he can never be certain that he is
awake. He cannot simply claim that, since God is no deceiver,
whenever he is convinced that he is awake, he has the right
to be certain that he is awake; for he may while dreaming
know that God exists and be convinced that he is awake. Nor
will it do for Descartes to say, "Since God is no deceiver, I
can be certain that on *most occasions* when I am convinced
that I am awake, I am awake." For, if he has no means of
distinguishing dreams from waking states, he cannot be justifiably certain on any occasion when he is convinced that he is

awake that he is in fact awake. Descartes requires nothing less than a criterion for distinguishing dreaming from waking and in fact in the *Sixth Meditation* he presents one:

And I ought to set aside all the doubts of these past days as hyperbolical and ridiculous, particularly that very common uncertainty respecting sleep, which I could not distinguish from the waking state; for at present I find a very notable difference between the two, inasmuch as our memory can never connect our dreams one with the other, or with the whole course of our lives, as it unites events which happen to us while we are awake. And, as a matter of fact, if someone, while I was awake quite suddenly appeared to me and disappeared as fast as do the images which I see in sleep, so that I could not know from whence the form came nor whither it went, it would not be without reason that I should deem it a spectre or a phantom formed by my brain [and similar to those which I form in sleep], rather than a real man. But when I perceive things as to which I know distinctly both the place from which they proceed, and that in which they are, and the time at which they appeared to me; and when, without any interruption, I can connect the perceptions which I have of them with the whole course of my life, I am perfectly assured that these perceptions occur while I am waking and not during sleep. And I ought in no wise to doubt the truth of such matters, if after having called up all my senses, my memory, and my understanding, to examine them, nothing is brought to evidence by any one of them which is repugnant to what is set forth by the others. For because God is in no wise a deceiver, it follows that I am not deceived in this.[23]

Several comments are in order regarding the above passage. In the *First Meditation*, Descartes considered coherence within an episode in his life, such as being seated by a fireplace in a nightgown and everything seeming to be taking place in accordance with the laws of nature, as possibly a criterion for knowing that he was awake. He rejected it, however, on the ground that dreams often duplicate coherent episodes. Presently it is not coherence within an episode but coherence between episodes which constitutes the criterion. All the episodes in one's life, which, so to speak, fit together are labeled "waking states"; and those which do not are labeled "dreams." For instance, I appear to witness events describable as traveling to Hofstra University, lecturing, driving home, going to sleep, dancing with witches on Mount Everest, getting up in the morning, and so on. It is because traveling to the university, lecturing, driving home, going to sleep, getting up in the morning, cohere between themselves and between all the remembered episodes of my past life that I label these experiences as "waking ones." On the other hand, because dancing with witches does not cohere with the episodes preceding it or succeeding it that I label it a "dream."

Second, Descartes is not merely stating how it is possible for a person who is in doubt that he is awake to justifiably convince himself that he is not dreaming. He is also stating why human beings when awake are convinced that they are. Obviously, a person rarely if ever asks himself, "Am I awake or dreaming?" and then proceeds to apply the above criterion to convince himself that he is awake. But, rather, because there is a continuity between waking experiences, though interrupted by intervals of dreaming, a person on most occasions automatically and unreflectively considers himself to be awake.

Third, Descartes allows that it is conceivable that coherence between episodes in his life is a criterion available to him but yet that he was never awake. This is possible because the same criterion which distinguishes waking from dreaming could possibly have distinguished within his life, which consists of one great big dream, those phases of it which are coherent from those which are not. His life, so to speak, might conceivably have been composed of unconnected short dreams within the context of a master dream. What is not conceivable is that a God who is no deceiver exists and that Descartes has a natural tendency to believe that the coherent episodes in his life consist of waking experiences when in fact they do not.

While Descartes' position in this matter appears to be plausible, it seems to me that it has one obvious shortcoming. Descartes cannot account for the fact that a person sometimes finds himself to be in a situation which he is unable to connect with the previous episodes of his life but yet is *justifiably* convinced that he is awake. For instance, according to an old tale, a beggar when in a drunken stupor was transported to the sultan's castle and on orders from the sultan was to be treated as the sultan. When the beggar awaked and, with amazement, looked about him, he at first thought he was dreaming. But upon pinching himself and talking to the guard, he very shortly became convinced that he was awake. He was, however, unable to connect his present situation as a sultan with his former life as a beggar. Now it seems to me, contrary to what is implied by Descartes' position, that the beggar's conviction that he was awake was as justified as my present conviction that I am writing in a notebook, though I have no problem of connecting my present situation with the previous episodes of my life. No doubt the ability to discover coherence is a sufficient condition for being justifiably certain that one is awake; what I question is that it is a necessary one. However, even if his conception of a criterion is too narrow, as I claim, Descartes did succeed in making his point; we often, when awake, know we are awake.

CHAPTER 9

Body and Mind

HAVING established the existence of the physical world, Descartes is now prepared to examine the relation between himself as a thinking being and a portion of this world to which he seems to be intimately connected and which he had in the past referred to as his body. In the *Second Meditation* he had discovered that he existed as a thinking thing; while he then did not know that physical bodies exist, he was uncertain, nevertheless, whether he could exist without a body. "Of course, one may wonder whether the nature which thinks," he writes to Henricus Reneri, "may perhaps be the same as the nature which occupies space, so that there is one nature which is both intellectual and corporeal..."[1] But in the *Sixth Meditation* he discovers that body and mind are distinct in the sense that he, as a thinking thing, can conceivably exist without his body. Descartes presents two arguments for this distinction.

I *Descartes' First Argument*

And first of all, because I know that all things which I apprehend clearly and distinctly can be created by God as I apprehend them, it suffices that I am able to apprehend one thing apart from another clearly and distinctly in order to be certain that the one is different from the other, since they may be made to exist in separation at least by the omnipotence of God; and it does not signify by what power this separation is made in order to compel me to judge them to be different: and therefore, just because I know certainly that I exist, and that meanwhile I do not remark that any other thing necessarily pertains to my nature or essence, excepting that I am a thinking thing, I rightly conclude that my essence consists solely in the fact that I am a thinking thing [or a substance whose whole essence or nature is to think]. And although possibly (or rather cer-

168

tainly, as I shall say in a moment) I possess a body with which I am very intimately conjoined, yet because, on the one side, I have a clear and distinct idea of myself inasmuch as I am only a thinking and unextended thing, and as, on the other, I possess a distinct idea of body, inasmuch as it is only an extended and unthinking thing, it is certain that this I [that is to say, my soul by which I am what I am], is entirely and absolutely distinct from my body and can exist without it.[2]

The above argument has three parts. In the first Descartes deals with the relationship between his clear and distinct perception and what God can do and presumably what He cannot do. Descartes cannot perceive figure apart from extension; hence (contrary to his teaching that God is the efficient cause of the eternal truths), God cannot create something which has a figure but is not extended. But if he can clearly and distinctly perceive himself as a thinking thing distinct from his body, then God can bring it about that he exists without a body. Notice, however, that Descartes does not say that when he clearly and distinctly perceives one thing apart from another he can therefore conclude that the two things exist separately. He says only that God can bring it about that they do. Descartes will very shortly discover that he is a man and that a man is a body and a mind intimately connected. The point that he implies at the very beginning of the argument is what he explicitly states at the end of it, namely, that he can exist without a body. His conclusion is clearly stated in the *Principles*:

And even if we suppose that God had united a body to a soul so closely that it was impossible to bring them together more closely, and made a single thing out of the two, they would yet remain really distinct one from the other notwithstanding the union; because however closely God connected them He could not set aside the power which He possessed of separating them, or conserving them one apart from the other, and those things which God can separate, or conceive in separation, are really distinct.[3]

In the second part of the argument, Descartes tries to demonstrate that thought is his essence: "I rightly conclude that my essence consists solely in the fact that I am a thinking thing." He grounds this conclusion on two premises: the first is that he exists, and the second is that he does not notice that any other thing pertains to his nature except that he is a thinking thing. Although the second premise does not appear to be self-evident, Descartes unfortunately does not supply us with a reason for accepting it. Probably what he had in mind was his discovery in the *Second Meditation* that he is a thing that thinks without knowing anything else about himself. From this he inferred that thought is both a necessary and sufficient condition for his existence. It is necessary, for should he cease to think he would cease to exist. For whatever else may be true about himself, he is certain that he must, in order to exist, be conscious of himself as an individual subsisting in time. And thought is also a sufficient condition; for, if nothing else were true about Descartes but the fact that he thinks and can say to himself, "I exist," that would be sufficient for him to exist.

But even granting that Descartes' essence is to think, it does not follow from this that he does not require a body in order to exist. It may be that thoughts are modes of certain kinds of bodies. What he tries to demonstrate in the third part of his argument is that this is not the case; that, in fact, thought belongs to one kind of substance and extension to another, which, though they may be intimately connected, are nevertheless distinct. He bases this conclusion on the premise that on the one hand he has a *distinct idea* of himself as a "thinking and unextended thing"; and on the other hand, an idea of a body, "inasmuch as it is only an extended and unthinking thing."

The term "distinct" has different connotations for Descartes. For instance, motion is distinct from extension; but since I cannot clearly and distinctly perceive something in motion without being extended, Descartes calls this distinction "modal." Again, substance and duration are distinct; but since substance cannot be conceived without duration, the distinction is what Descartes calls a "distinction of reason." And then there is a real distinction, which Descartes claims to perceive in the above argument between body and mind. In the *Principles,* Descartes states what he means by a "real distinction": "The *real* is properly speaking found between two or more substances; and we can conclude that two substances are really distinct one from the other from the sole fact that we can conceive the one clearly and distinctly without the other."[4]

But how can Descartes be certain that the distinction which he perceives between thought and extension is a real distinction and not a modal one? True, he does not perceive any necessary connection between a thing that thinks and one that is extended, but he surely cannot conclude from this that there is a real distinction between them. For it is one thing not to perceive a connection and another to perceive that there is none. What I have just stated is precisely what was involved in Arnauld's famous criticism of Descartes' argument in which he employed for his purpose an example from geometry:

Let us assume that a certain man is quite sure that the angle in a semicircle is a right angle and that hence the triangle made by this angle and the diameter is right-angled, but suppose he questions and has not yet firmly apprehended, nay, let us imagine that, misled by some fallacy, he denies that the square on its base is equal to the squares on the sides of the right-angled triangle. Now, according to our author's reasoning, he will see himself confirmed in his false belief. . . .

[For he will reason as follows:] since I know that all things I clearly and distinctly understand can be created by God just as I conceive them to exist, it is sufficient for me, in order to be sure that one thing is distinct from another, to be able to comprehend the one clearly and distinctly apart from the other, because it can be isolated by God. But I clearly and distinctly understand that this triangle is right-angled, without comprehending that the square on its base is equal to the squares on its sides. Hence God at least can create a right-angled triangle, the square on the base of which is not equal to the squares on its sides.[5]

Descartes, in answering Arnauld, distinguishes an adequate from a complete idea. An idea to be adequate "must embrace *all* the properties which exist in the thing known." No human being could ever know, except by a divine revelation, that he had an adequate idea even if in fact he had one. There may be properties of matter which no natural philosopher will ever discover. Only God both has adequate ideas and knows that he has them. But an idea to be complete need have only sufficient adequacy "To let us see that we have not rendered it inadequate by an intellectual abstraction." Ideas such as figure, motion, and doubt are inadequate as candidates for existent things because they were formed by means of abstraction. Not so a complete idea, for the latter involves a conception sufficient to inform the mind that the idea signifies "an entity in itself and diverse from every other."[6]

Arnauld failed, according to Descartes, to make the distinction between an adequate and a complete idea. Therefore he insisted that nothing less than an adequate idea of mind and body is required in order to make a real distinction between them. But this requirement is erroneous; all that is required is a complete idea. I have sufficient knowledge of a thing that thinks, says Descartes, to be certain that it was not rendered inadequate by abstraction and, consequently, that such an entity can exist without requiring corporeal properties. As for Arnauld's example of a triangle, Descartes took some issue with him on how we may correctly conceive a triangle; but his main point is that, although a triangle may be taken in the concrete as a substance which has a triangular shape, the property of having the square on the base equal to the squares on the sides is obviously not a substance. Therefore, unlike the body and the mind, there can be no complete knowledge of it.[7]

Descartes did not adequately meet Arnauld's criticism. There are only three ways in which Descartes could possibly be certain that there is a real distinction between body and mind along the lines of his present argument. First, there is at least one property X which is essential for a body to exist and a property Y which is essential in order for a substance that thinks to exist, and Descartes clearly perceives that nothing could conceivably exist which has both X and Y. Descartes could not avail himself of this strategy since, according to his position, he as a human being is a substantial union of body-mind. Second, Descartes knows that he has an adequate idea of a thing that thinks and perceives that no corporeal property is contained in his idea. This will not do, because Descartes claims that, even if a human being were to have an adequate idea, he could never, except by the intervention of God, know that he had one. Third, Descartes has an adequate criterion for distinguishing a complete from an incomplete idea. As a result of applying the criterion, he perceives that his idea of a thinking substance without corporeal properties is a complete idea. Again, this will not do, since Descartes presents us with no criterion in his answer to Arnauld but merely says that he clearly perceives that the idea of himself as a thinking thing is complete. But how can he be certain that he has not rendered his idea inadequate? "May there not," as Anthony Kenny says, "be some necessary relationship, unsuspected by Descartes, that will link his idea of a thinking substance to that of an extended body?"[8]

Perhaps Descartes has a criterion for identifying a complete idea which he did not mention in his reply to Arnauld. A person has a complete idea of a thing when he detects its leading property, that is, essence; and he knows that he has detected the latter when there are a series of modes which he perceives to be different manifestations of the leading property. Thought is a leading attribute of himself, since there are a manifold of different modes such as believing, doubting, desiring, feeling, and so on which belong to him and are different manifestations of thought. And extension is a leading attribute of body, since shape, size, divisibility, and so on are different manifestations of extension. With this point in mind, Descartes' argument can be formulated as follows:

(1) thought is a leading property of myself as a thinking substance;
(2) extension is a leading property of my body;
(3) a substance can only have one leading property;
(4) consequently, there is a real distinction between my mind and body.

The weakness of this argument is that Descartes discovers (3), namely that a substance can have only one leading property (essence), as a result of perceiving the real distinction between body and mind. Consequently, he cannot use (3) to establish this distinction, for to do so is to reason in a circle.

II *Descartes' Second Argument*

Toward the end of the *Sixth Meditation*, Descartes presents a second argument for the mind-body distinction:

. . . There is a great difference between mind and body, inasmuch as body is by nature always divisible and the mind is entirely indivisible. For, as a matter of fact, when I consider the mind, that is to say, myself inasmuch as I am only a thinking thing, I cannot distinguish in myself any parts, but apprehend myself to be clearly one and entire; and although the whole mind seems to be united to the whole body, yet if a foot, or an arm, or some other part, is separated from my body, I am aware that nothing has been taken away from my mind. And the faculties of willing, feeling, conceiving, etc. cannot be properly speaking said to be its parts, for it is one and the same mind which employs itself in willing and in feeling and understanding. But it is quite otherwise with corporeal or extended objects, for there is not one of these imaginable by me which my mind cannot easily divide into parts, and which consequently I do not recognize as being divisible; this would be sufficient to teach me that the mind or soul of man is entirely different from the body, if I had not already learned it from other sources.[9]

It is apparent from the last remark in this quotation that Descartes considered this argument to be distinct from the previous one. The argument is based on the premise that a body has parts whereas a thinking substance has faculties but no parts. Descartes' attempt, however, at showing where the difference lies between faculties and parts is misleading. He says, "for it is one and the same mind which employs itself in willing and in feeling and understanding"; on the other hand, in the case of bodies, "there is not one imaginable by me which my mind cannot easily divide into parts." But one might correctly say of a body what Descartes said of the mind: "For it is one and the same body which employs itself in running, breathing, saluting and so on." The significant point about bodies in this matter is that a part of a body is itself a body. "Thus," writes Descartes elsewhere, "the hand is an incomplete substance, when taken in relation with the body of which it is a part; but regarded alone it is a complete substance."[10] On the other hand, willing, feeling, and conceiving, as faculties of the mind, are not thinking substances. There is no doubt that Descartes is right in making this distinction between the parts of the body and the faculties of the mind, but is this a sufficient basis for drawing a real distinction between body and mind? I think not. Let us formulate the argument in the form of a simple syllogism:

(1) I as a subject that thinks am not composed of parts;
(2) my body is composed of parts;
(3) hence, I as a subject that thinks am not a body.

The conclusion follows from the premises, and the second premise is obviously true; but the first seems to me to beg the point at issue. For the materialist will simply deny the premise on the ground that there is no real distinction between the subject that thinks and the body which is composed of parts, and will assert that, consequently, contrary to (1), I as a subject that thinks am composed of parts.

It might be said that Descartes is not exposed to the above criticism, having used the expression "when I consider the mind, that is to say, myself inasmuch as I am only a thinking thing, I cannot distinguish in myself any parts. . . ." This expression is, however, ambiguous and could mean (a) when I consider myself as a thinking substance without considering my other properties, I cannot distinguish in myself any parts; or (b) when I consider myself as a substance whose *sole* nature is to think without considering my other properties, I cannot distinguish in myself any parts. Obviously (a) can be true. I can always attend to some mode of a substance without concerning myself with its other modes. I can, for instance, consider myself as a substance who dances without considering my other properties such as my hope for peace, my ability to think abstractly, and so on. But if proposition (a) were substituted for (1) in the above argument, the conclusion would not follow from the premises. Analogously, I can meaningfully think of a body in motion without considering its size and shape, but I surely cannot use this thought as a premise to arrive at a conclusion that there is a real distinction between the former and the latter. On the other hand, proposition (b) can be used to arrive at the desired conclusion. Unfortunately (b) is simply a restatement of (1) and begs the point at issue.

The expression in the passage, "Yet if a foot, or an arm, or some other part, is separated from my body, I am aware that nothing has been taken away from my mind," suggests another but related argument to the one above. Let us introduce the following terms: "contingently dispensable and indispensable" and "logically dispensable and indispensable." A materialist will claim that, unlike my foot or arm, my brain is contingently indispensable for my existence in the sense that I cannot exist without a functioning brain; but he would have to confess that my brain is logically dispensable in the sense that I can *conceivably* exist without a brain. The world might have been radically different from what it is and persons like myself might have existed without brains. Descartes' argument is then as follows: (1) there is no part of my body which is logically indispensable respecting my existence as a thinking being; (2) my body is the sum of its parts; (3) hence, my body is logically dispensable respecting my existence as a thing that thinks.

I am inclined to believe that the conclusion of the above argument, even if true, does not establish that mind and body are distinct substances. For (3) is not synonymous with the proposition "I can conceivably exist without a body"; it merely says "I could conceivably exist without the body that I have." The continuity of my existence, even for a materialist, need not depend on my having the same body throughout my existence. My friend and I could conceivably wake up one morning with our bodies exchanged: I now tall and blond, he short and dark. I do not think that a materialist has to rule this possibility out as conceivable. He could maintain that the continuity of the self is the continuity of thought, memory, and personality and not that of an identical body. This conclusion is in no way inconsistent with the proposition that no one could conceivably think without a body. Moreover, I do not believe the argument is a good one, for while the premises are true, the conclusion does not follow from the premises. What I can conclude from the premises is that there is no part of my body which is logically indispensable, but not that all of them collectively are dispensable. I can logically dispense with my liver or my heart or my brain and so on, but not necessarily with all of them at the same time.

III   *The Body-mind Complex*

In the previous chapter, we saw that Descartes discovered that he had a body by considering what nature had taught him regarding his brain images and sensations. And now, believing that he has established that his mind is distinct from his body, he claims that nature teaches him that they are so intimately connected as to form a substantial union:

Nature also teaches me by these sensations of pain, hunger, thirst, etc., that I am not only lodged in my body as a pilot in a vessel, but that I am very closely united to it, and so to speak so intermingled with it that I seem to compose with it one whole. For if that were not the case, when my body is hurt, I who am merely a thinking thing, should not feel pain, for I should perceive this wound by the understanding only, just as the sailor perceives by sight when something is damaged in his vessel; and when my body has need of drink or food, I should clearly understand the fact without being warned of it by confused feelings of hunger and thirst. For all these sensations of hunger, thirst, pain, etc., are in truth none other than certain confused modes of thought which are produced by the union and apparent intermingling of mind and body.[11]

This passage is one of the most significant in the *Meditations*, for it records Descartes' discovery that he is a human being whose essence is a body and mind intimately connected. Bear in mind that the *Meditations* is essentially a journal of self-discovery. Descartes' first discovery, after adopting a position of universal doubt, is that he exists as a thing that thinks; then that he is a finite substance whose existence is dependent on God; and now that he is man. There is, however, a significant difference between Descartes' first two discoveries about himself and his last. He learned that he existed as a finite being and that God exists by the clear and distinct ideas which belong to his understanding. But that he is a man he learned from *the fact* that he has "certain confused modes of thought," that is, sensations which provide him with privileged, though confused, access to certain occurrences in his body. They are confused in two respects. While nature has taught human beings that certain sensations signify certain occurrences in their bodies, they are nevertheless sometimes misled by them.

A person, for instance, occasionally feels hungry when his body has no need for food. Second, while sensations are mental states which have physical causes, we have a natural tendency to locate them in bodies and to attribute to these bodies properties which resemble them. Thus, a person locates his pain in his left hand or attributes to the fire a property which resembles his sensation of heat.[12]

A person's body and mind, according to Descartes, are incomplete substances relative to his being a man just as the hand is an incomplete substance relative to the body. Incomplete in a sense, but, nevertheless, a substance, for a severed hand can exist unattached to the body. Likewise a mind can exist without a body and a body without a mind, "Quite in the same way [like the hand relative to the body] mind and body are incomplete substances viewed in relation to the man who is the unity which together they form; but taken alone, they are complete."[13]

There are, however, two significant differences between mind and body relative to a person's existence. When a person dies and there is no longer a connection between his mind and body, the mind, if it survives, is the person but not the body. Descartes would not deny that his having been born with a human body is one of his essential properties, but he would insist that his continued existence does not depend on his body, whereas his being a mind must essentially be true of him throughout his existence. Before Descartes discovered that he was a man, he knew that whatever else may have been essential for his being the person he was, his ability at present and at some time in the future to think was both a necessary and sufficient condition for his continued existence. Why was Descartes so certain of this? Surely, the fact that he is a man and that a man is a body and mind intimately connected would seem to suggest that, if, so to speak, the two substances of which he was composed were to part company, he would then cease to exist. To answer this question we must again consider the *Cogito* argument. This argument did not, as Descartes himself pointed out, establish that he could exist without a body; but it did demonstrate that if such a possibility were conceivable, then he would remain Descartes, notwithstanding the fact that he was no longer a human being. And the reason is that, in presenting the *Cogito* argument, he knew only that he was a substance that thinks, and since he could not doubt his existence, he felt certain that nothing more was required for him to exist than the ability to think and present the *Cogito* argument. Second, Descartes' reason for referring to a portion of the physical world as "my body" is because of its intimate connection with his mind, but the converse does not hold. He does not identify a certain mind as being his own on the ground that it is intimately connected with his body. Again, this point can be learned from the *Cogito* argument. For the latter demonstrated that Descartes' indubitable conviction of the occurrence of any thought was sufficient for his immediate identification of himself as being the subject who does the thinking.

The above matter can be stated in another way. The question "Why do I call a particular mind as 'my mind' " is pointless, for in the very act of posing this question I identify my mind as the very mind which posed it. Not so the question "Why do I call a certain part of the physical universe as 'my body?' "; for, in the above passage, Decartes supplies an answer to this question: "I am very closely united to it and so to speak intermingled with it that I seem to compose with it one whole." Considering the two matters above, I think we can conclude that, while Descartes is a man and, as a man, his body is as necessary for his existence as is his mind, nevertheless, his mind is more significant than his body respecting his existence.

In the above quoted passage, Descartes' conclusion that he is a man is based on a contrast between what would have been the case if his mind and body did not form a quasi-substantial unity and what is actually the case, namely, his being a man. For, if I were not a man, says Descartes, "... when *my body* is hurt, I who am merely a thinking thing should not feel pain, for I should perceive this wound by the understanding only ..." What could Descartes, in this passage, have meant by "my body"? He could not have meant the body in which my mind is spatially located as the pilot is located in his ship. For Descartes' mind is a substance whose nature is only to think (using "thought" in Descartes' broad sense);

conequently, not only could it not occupy space but it could not be spatially located. Nor is it likely that Descartes meant by his body, the area of the physical world which he has *direct* control over, in the sense that he could move his arm, legs, and head directly, whereas in order to move a stick or throw a stone he first has to move his limbs. Descartes seems to have played down the significance of bodily agency in his treatment of the relationship between his body and mind. To Reneri he writes:

It does not seem to me a fiction, but a truth which nobody should deny, that there is nothing entirely in our power except our thoughts; at least if you take the word "thought" as I do, to cover all the operations of the soul. . . . In philosophical language there is nothing strictly attributable to a man apart from what is covered by the word "thought"; for the activities which belong to the body alone are said to take place in a man rather than to be performed by him.[14]

There are two reasons which led Descartes to adopt this position. First, as he says further in the letter, external things are only partially in our power but not "absolutely and completely." I can, for instance, will to move my arm and then discover that I cannot do so. I may be paralyzed or my arm may be under the control of some invisible power. Second and more significant—and what most likely led Descartes to say that with respect to his body a man is not an agent—is that when he intends to raise his arm, he does not immediately bring it about; on the contrary, intervening between his intention and the raising of his arm, there are a series of events which take place in his brain, nerves, and muscles which make it possible for him to raise his arm. These things clearly are not performances, even in the loose sense in which one might say that Descartes moves his arm but are rather things that happen to him like his eye dilations and muscle contractions.

What Descartes most likely had in mind when he used the term "my body" to refer to what would have been the case if his mind was not intimately connected with his body, was first of all the pineal gland, which might be called "the soul's window to the physical world." Now, since the pineal gland belongs to the brain and is part of a single functional system which includes the heart, muscles, limbs, and so on, the latter is included under the designation "my body." According to Descartes, the mind, that is, the understanding, directly perceives the physical patterns generated in the pineal gland and indirectly the bodies which correspond in external space with these patterns. Descartes advocates a doctrine of representative perception, but as Norman Kemp Smith says, "...the correspondence to be established is no longer between objects assumed to be mental, and physical bodies, but between brain patterns (ideas *corporeas*) and the distant bodies mechanically generative of them..."[15] Now, if Descartes was not intimately connected with his body, as the above passage from the *Sixth Mediation* indicates, then the *only* acquaintance his mind could possibly have with the physical universe, including his own body, is as a result of his understanding perceiving the patterns in his pineal gland. He would have no privileged access to occurrences within his body; for the only way he could know about them is by means of his brain patterns, whose likenesses could be perceived by some other mind in his own respective pineal gland. I could perceive my split finger in no different way than my neighbor could perceive it. We both visually see it. (Perception for Descartes is an act of the understanding: "It is the soul that sees and not the eye...."[16]) This is what Descartes meant above when he says, "I should perceive this wound by the understanding only, just as the sailor perceives by sight when something is damaged in his vessel." The point is that since he can not possibly, by feeling, detect that his body is damaged, he can do so only visually by the understanding.

But, as Descartes says, I am a man, and not merely a thinking ego, but a mind and body intimately connected; therefore, the above characterization of "my body" is inadequate. I have feelings of pain, hunger, thirst, and so on which inform me about certain conditions in my body and which constitute a kind of "knowledge" about my body which is not available to anyone else. My body is not a mere mechanistic system which produces physical patterns to be inspected by the understanding, but rather I am intimately connected with all the parts of my body and "seem to compose with it one whole." Sensations signify this intimacy; for, unlike physical patterns which originate solely from physical causes, and unlike concepts which belong to a mind, irrespective as to whether it is embodied or disembodied, sensations "arise from the union and, as it were, the intermixture of mind and body."

CHAPTER 10

Two Problems about the Mind and the Body

TWO problems relating to the mind and the body do not appear in the *Meditations* but, from a logical point of view, they belong after our discussion of man as an intimate union of mind and body. In philosophical literature, they have been called "the mind-body problem" and "the problem of other minds."

Let us first consider "the mind-body problem." In the *Meditations*, Descartes speaks of hunger, thirst, and pain as "certain confused modes of thought" which are brought about by certain states of the body. He also, throughout his writings, speaks of how the mind brings about certain events in the brain, nerves, and muscles. Descartes, in this matter, is in agreement with common sense, that some physical events are caused by mental events and, conversely, some mental events by physical ones. This position is called "interactionism." Many philosophers, however, have felt that Descartes faces a serious problem by adopting interactionism. Thus, Anthony Kenny writes: "On Descartes' principles it is *difficult* to see how an unextended thinking substance can cause motion in an extended unthinking substance and how the extended unthinking substance can cause sensations in the unextended thinking substance. The properties of the two kinds of substance seem to place them in such diverse categories that it is *impossible* for them to interact."[1] Kenny's remark is puzzling; for if Descartes' conceptions of mind and body precludes the possibility of interaction, as Kenny's second sentence implies, then there can be no difficult problem of how it is possible for mind and body to interact, which his first sentence implies. When something is impossible, there can be no difficult problem as to how it is possible. Kenny is not unique in his unclear presentation of the mind-body problem. A lack of clarity characterizes most of the writing on this topic by both Descartes' followers and critics. The reason is that this so-called "problem" is really a pseudoproblem; for, when someone introduces it, he presupposes three things:

(1) there can be no causal interaction between two radically different substances;

(2) mind and body are radically different substances; and

(3) the mind acts on the body and the body on the mind.

The three propositions above form an inconsistent triad in that, while any two of the above sentences can be true, all three cannot. Descartes, in accepting (2) and (3) rejects (1); what point can there then be in saying that Descartes has a difficult problem as to how body and mind can interact, for in rejecting (1) he eliminates a necessary presupposition for raising the problem.

Descartes first addressed himself to the issue of interactionism in his letters to Princess Elizabeth and later in the *Passions of the Soul*. In his letter to Elizabeth of May, 1643, Descartes claimed that human knowledge is grounded on certain "primitive notions" and that we are mistaken if we try to explain one of these notions by another; for, since they are primitive, each of them can only be understood by itself. Among the primitive notions, he lists not only soul (mind) and body but also the union between them. "Finally," he concludes, "as regards soul and body together, we have only the notion of their union, on which depends our notion of the soul's power to move the body, and the body's power to act on the soul and cause sensations and passions."[2] What is significant about Descartes' conception of the mind-body union, on which his notion of interactionism depends, is that it cannot be analyzed into the distinct conceptions of mind and body. I cannot, as the result of my clear and distinct idea of soul and that of body, clearly perceive the nature of their union. The latter is as primitive and fundamental as that of soul and body.[3] For Descartes, therefore, there can be no problem as to how it is possible for such radically different natures as soul and body to form a union; for in posing such a problem, one is pre-supposing that the concept of their union is not a primitive notion.

In a subsequent letter to Princess Elizabeth, Descartes claims that, unlike his notions of body and mind, the notion of their union is derived from "the ordinary course of life":

First of all then, I observe one great difference between these three kinds of notions. The soul can be conceived only by pure intellect; the body (i.e., extension, shape, and movement) can likewise be known by pure intellect, but much better by intellect aided by imagination; and finally what belongs to the union of the soul and the body can be known only obscurely by pure intellect or by intellect aided by imagination, but it can be known very clearly by the senses. That is why people who never philosophize and use only their senses have no doubt that the soul moves the body and that the body acts on the soul. They regard both of them as a single thing. . . .[4]

Descartes is not saying that it is because human reason is limited, that the union of the soul and the body cannot, like the body or the soul, be known by the pure intellect; and that consequently we have to settle in accepting their union on the basis of the senses. His position is rather that their union could not conceivably be known by the pure intellect. There simply is no necessary connection between the sensation of pain in the soul and damage in the body or between the soul's feeling of hunger and the body's need for food. In order to have a clear perception of these relations, and consequently conceive the mind-body union, the intellect must, so to speak, turn away from the objects of the understanding and turn instead to the passions and sensations which occur to a man in the course of his daily life. Descartes adds: "But it is the ordinary course of life and conversation, and abstention from meditation and from the study of the things which exercise the imagination, that teaches us how to conceive the union of the soul and the body."[5]

In the *Passions of the Soul*, Descartes returns to the subject of mind-body interaction, but this time his concern is not with the source of the knowledge of the interaction but rather with the manner in which it takes place. He says there that while the mind is united to the whole body, there is yet a part of it in which the soul exercises its functions immediately.[6] This part is the pineal gland which he held to be situated in the middle of the brain. Descartes is not here referring merely to the physical patterns located in the gland which is perceived by the intellect; for as we had seen previously, even if the mind and body were not intimately connected, such patterns might have been present to the understanding. He is referring to all causal interactions between the soul and the body, including those involving sensations and passions. The pineal gland, so to speak, is not only the window to the physical world but the place where the mind and the body exchange messages: "Let us then conceive here that the soul has its principal seat in the little gland which exists in the middle of the brain, from whence it radiates forth through all the remainder of the body by means of the animal spirits, nerves, and even the blood, which, participating in the impressions of the spirits, can carry them by the arteries into all the members."[7] Descartes gave this privileged status to the pineal gland, because he believed that with the exception of this gland, all the other parts of the brain are double and, consequently, could not be used to explain how the two images, each in one eye, which is caused by the reflection of light, becomes one image.[8]

We know today that Descartes was mistaken in claiming that the pineal gland is "the seat of the soul." His general procedure was, however, correct; for once mind-body interaction is accepted, then the only relevant problem concerns the functional mechanism which makes interactionism possible. Descartes tried to find an answer to this question and failed; but he is not exposed to the criticism, which is often leveled against him, of having evaded "the real mind-body problem."

I The Problem of Other Minds

Having discovered that he is a mind-body complex and that there are many other bodies besides his own, Descartes asks himself whether any of these other bodies are intimately connected with finite minds. To solve it Descartes obviously has to have a criterion in order to distinguish bodies with minds

from those which have none. The first criterion which he thought
of is that those bodies who behave in ways similar to his own
are persons and those who do not are mindless. For instance,
the likelihood is that a body which initiates its own motions in
order to flee from a situation where its bodily integrity is
threatened possesses a mind. Despite the seeming plausibility
of this criterion, Descartes rejected it on the ground that most
of the actions he performs, including those which are suitable
to situations he finds himself to be in, are done automatically
without his consciously attending to them. To the Marquess
of Newcastle, Descartes writes: "It often happens that we
walk or eat without thinking at all about what we are doing;
and similarly without using our reason, we reject things which
are harmful for us and parry the blows aimed at us."[9] Given
this latter fact, there is the possibility that there exist self-moving
complex machines, whose behavior resembles Descartes' own,
but, unlike Descartes, thought and consciousness form no part
of the causes of their actions.[10] Descartes felt that what he
required was criteria in order to distinguish persons from
pure automata, or what we today call "robots."

In the *Discourse* he presents two such criteria:

The first is, that they [the pure automata] never use speech or other
signs as we do when placing our thoughts on record for the benefit
of others. . . . But it never happens that it [the pure automaton]
arranges its speech in various ways, in order to reply appropriately
to everything that may be said in its presence, as even the lowest
type of man can do.[11]

Descartes is not denying that a pure automaton can utter words
or even sentences; for, as he indicates in the same passage, a
machine can be so constructed that if it is touched in one part
of its body, it might emit sounds which take the form of the
question, "What do you want from me?" But what it cannot
do, says Descartes, is to respond appropriately to a variety of
questions that are presented to it. Descartes' second criterion is:

And the second difference is, that although machines can perform
certain things as well as or perhaps better than any of us can do,
they infallibly fall short in others, by which means we may discover

that they did not act from knowledge, but only from the disposition of their organs. For while reason is a universal instrument which can serve for all contingencies, these organs have need of some special adaptation for every particular action. From this it follows that it is morally impossible that there should be sufficient diversity in any machine to allow it to act in all the events of life in the same way as our reason causes us to act.[12]

A machine, whether it is a natural machine like a dog (Descartes, as we shall shortly see, held that animals are pure automata) or an artificial machine like a dancing doll, might do certain things better than a human; but it will show itself to be a machine because the range of its abilities is very small compared to those of the dullest human beings.

If one accepts the labels of Keith Gunderson,[13] Descartes' first test for distinguishing between persons and machines should be called "the language test" and the second, "the action test." The word "test" is appropriate, for these tests are the means by which Descartes is able to ascertain who is a person and who is a pure automaton. The only bodies Descartes discovers to pass his tests are those that resemble him very closely in bodily form and behavior, and which, since childhood, he has referred to as humans. On the other hand, all animals, including those who, like baboons and apes, resemble humans in bodily structure and appearance, fail his tests; therefore he considers them to be pure automata devoid of any consciousness and thought. There is, however, a difference between the two tests. Descartes never abandoned the action test; but it is clear, however, that he held the language test to be superior. In his famous letter to More, he contends that only by means of the language test can one be sure of any given body that it belongs to a person: "Such speech is the only certain sign of thought hidden in a body."[14]

Why did Descartes consider the language test superior to the action test? He provides us with no explicit answer to this question. We can, however, formulate an answer on his behalf from the things he does say. In stating why the action test is appropriate, Descartes says: "For while reason is a universal instrument which can serve for all contingencies, these organs

[Descartes is here referring to the organs of pure automata] have need for some special adaptation for every particular action."[15] Let us call this statement "Descartes' principle." The principle provides the ground for both the action and the language tests and can be stated as follows: a pure automaton, in order to respond relevantly to a set of situations, linguistic or otherwise, must be directly programmed to do so, whereas a thinking automaton is programmed with an ability to formulate his own relevant responses to all possible situations. A sheep, for instance, has been programmed by nature so that when light is reflected from the body of a wolf and enters his eyes, he will automatically and immediately flee. A human, insofar as he is an automaton, also has the tendency to flee at the sight of a wolf; however, being a thinking substance, he need not automatically flee but may, thanks to his reason, devise some relevant response to the situation other than fleeing. I have used the term "relevant" in formulating Descartes' principle, because what is required in order to test an automaton, as to whether it is a pure or a thinking one, is not whether it responds appropriately to situations but whether it does so relevantly. An appropriate response is relevant but the converse need not be true. For instance, people who walk out of a burning movie house in an orderly manner respond appropriately to the situation; but, if they rush out like a herd of steers, they are responding relevantly but not appropriately; if they sit in their seats conversing about aesthetics, then they are responding irrelevantly.

In order to show the difference in the application of Descartes' principle to both tests which accounts for the superiority of the language test, let us reintroduce Descartes' demon; moreover, let us suppose that Descartes is the sole thinking self-moving body in the universe and that in order to deceive him the demon has constructed a race of robots who are similar to Descartes in both appearance and behavior. Now the demon, knowing the laws of nature, the composition of the earth, and all that occurs in it, can anticipate all the possible kinds of situations his robots will confront, with the exception of linguistic ones. Consequently, he is able to program them so that they can respond relevantly to all nonlinguistic contingencies. In other words, they can pass the action test. They can not, however, pass the language test! To see why they cannot, let us introduce the concept of linguistic competence. An individual is linguistically competent if he satisfies the following two conditions:

(1) he can use sentences meaningfully in order to convey information to others; and

(2) he can respond relevantly to novel sentences, namely, sentences which he was not directly programmed to respond to and which were never uttered in his presence.

Now (1) logically entails that he is a person; and (2) does not. However, Descartes believes that an individual's ability to respond to novel sentences constitutes a sufficient ground for claiming that (1) applies to him as well and that consequently he possesses a mind. Why? Because languages like English, French, and Latin are sufficiently rich so that there is no limit to the number of syntactically correct sentences that can be generated in any one of them. This should be apparent when one considers that almost, if not all, the sentences written in this work, with the exception of quotations, have never been seen or heard by anyone else. Now, since there is no limit to the number of French or Latin sentences, the demon cannot program his robots so that they can respond relevantly to all the possible sentences which Descartes can utter in their presence. At some point in talking to these pure automata Descartes will cease being deceived; for, since they have failed his language test, he will conclude that they are mere machines.

II *Animals are Pure Automata*

On the basis of the language test, Descartes concluded that human beings have minds but that animals are pure automata. But why pure automata? One would, on the face of it, have assumed that the language test only disqualified animals as being capable of forming concepts and making judgments. Why should Descartes have used it also to deny that animals have sensations and feelings? His position in this matter is, after all, so contrary to common sense as to sound paradoxical. According to some commentators, what led Descartes to deny sensations to animals was his position that sensations are confused modes of thinking. Thus Zeno Vendler writes: "Our concept of thought is restricted to a part of this domain, namely to mental acts, states and processes with propositional content. Descartes, as far as I can see, never succeeded in catching this distinction and to him sensation remained a sort of 'confused' thinking."[16] On one point Vendler is undoubtedly right; sensations are radically different from thoughts. Thoughts are propositional in nature, sensations are not. "I am in pain" is true or false, but my sensation of pain is neither. Vendler also *seems* to be right in attributing to Descartes the position that sensations are confused modes of thinking. "... These sensations," writes Descartes, "of hunger, thirst, pain, etc., are in truth none other than certain confused modes of thought...."[17]

Nevertheless, I do not accept Vendler's claim that Descartes failed to distinguish propositional thoughts from sensations, and that consequently he was led to deny that animals have sensations. (Descartes often uses the word "thought" broadly to signify "all that of which we are conscious as operating in us." In this broad sense, sensations, though nonpropositional, are thoughts.) Descartes, as indicated previously, held a kind of signal theory of sensations. Pain is a signal from the body to the mind that it is damaged; hunger that it requires food. Now, while the feelings of pain and hunger do not have propositional content, what they signify is expressed propositionally; in the one case, it is that the body is damaged; and in the other, that it is in need of food. The propositional thought and the judgment are, however, distinct; for the judgment is an act of the will which consents to or denies the proposition. Descartes' position, it seems to me, is that while the sensation and its accompanying thought are distinct, the awareness of the former cannot occur without the latter. I cannot consciously feel pain without entertaining the proposition that something is wrong with my body. I need not accept the proposition, in the sense of judging it to be true, but I cannot fail to entertain it insofar as I am aware of the sensation. I have used above the terms "being conscious," and "being aware of the sensation"; for a man may have a pain of low intensity and not be aware of it, because he concentrates his mind on something else. And obviously we often fail to take notice of sensations which

signify events about external bodies. People often walk con-
centrating their minds on some subject matter without being
aware of the sounds, smells, and visual sensations which they
are experiencing. Descartes would, however, quite rightly insist
that no self-regulating machine can possibly have sensations
without being capable of being aware of them.

It follows from what I have said above that Descartes did
not confuse sensations with propositional thoughts but rather
that his position was that no automaton can possibly experience
sensations unless it is capable of entertaining propositions. And
when, in the above quotation, and elsewhere, he speaks of
sensations as "confused modes of thought," it is not, strictly
speaking, the sensations which are confused but the thoughts
which inevitably accompany them. The sensation of pain is
neither clear nor confused, but when I entertain the thought
that my sensation is located spatially in the damaged part of
my body, then my thought is a confused one. Now, if I am
right in this matter, then Vendler's reason for Descartes' denying sensations to animals is mistaken. In my interpretation,
Descartes' reason was that no automaton can experience sensations without the ability to entertain propositions; consequently,
since animals are incapable of the latter, they cannot experience sensations.

Descartes' case for the position that animals are pure automata
is not confined to their failure to pass the language test; he
has two other significant reasons, both of which are found in
his letter to More. His first reason is that all the motions of
animal bodies can be adequately explained by a bodily mechanism: "I soon saw clearly that they could all originate from
the corporeal and mechanical principle, and I thenceforward
regard it as certain and established that we can not at all
prove the presence of a thinking soul in animals."[18] Descartes
did not consider the fact that animal behavior, in many respects,
resembles our own and often seems clever and ingenious, as
constituting *a strong case* for their having sensations and
thoughts. "I am not disturbed," he writes, "by the astuteness
and cunning of dogs and foxes, or all the things which animals
do for the sake of food, sex, and fear; I claim that I can easily
explain the origin of all of them from the constitution of their

organs."[19] The key phrase in the above quotation is "for the sake of food, sex, and fear." There is a fundamental difference, according to Descartes, between humans and animals. The latter are solely biological entities; humans are cultural as well. (Descartes never used this terminology, but, I believe, that in this context, it aptly describes what he wants to say.) Descartes, in this argument, is contending that purely biological entities are most likely pure automata on the ground that biological and psychological explanations for animal behavior can in *all cases* be replaced by mechanical explanations in which nothing is employed but physical-object terminology. He believed that in his physiological studies he had already done much toward accomplishing this task. On the other hand, he could not explain the cultural activities of human beings, such as their use of language, their ability to build complex machines, and their religious and scientific activities unless he attributed to them minds like his own.

The above is a formidable argument if the so-called "goods," namely, the mechanical explanations for animal behavior, can be delivered. We know today that Descartes was over-optimistic in this matter, though many scientists and philosophers today claim that his vision of a science of animal behavior, which would be a branch of physics, will most likely be achieved in the near future.

Descartes' second argument, in his letter to More, is very short. He writes: "... it is more probable that worms and flies and caterpillars move mechanically than that they all have immortal souls."[20] True, but what about baboons and dolphins—why might not some animals have immortal souls and others not? To this Descartes has a reply in his letter to Newcastle: "... There is no reason to believe it of some animals without believing it of all, and many of them such as oysters and sponges are too imperfect for this to be credible."[21] Descartes' position, considering the above two quotations, is as follows: it has been held that baboons and chimpanzees think and have sensations on the ground that their organs and behavior resemble our own. This argument, however, proves too much; for, suppose we accept the conclusion that higher primates have souls. It would then be unreasonable to deny it to lower ones, such as monkeys, for the difference in conduct and bodily structure between baboons and monkeys is not sufficiently great to warrant attributing souls to one and not the other. But, if we attribute it to monkeys, then again, and for the same reason, it would be unreasonable not to attribute souls to all other mammals. And, if to mammals, why not to alligators and so on. Finally, we end up with oysters and sponges, which belong to the lowest tier in the animal kingdom. There is simply no place in the hierarchy of animals where a clear boundary can be drawn between those who have souls from those who have not, for the continuity between them renders it unreasonable that we make this distinction between them. Consequently, in accepting the argument from analogy between humans and higher primates, we have to conclude that all animals have souls; but, unfortunately, it is highly unlikely that oysters and sponges have them.

We thus confront three exhaustive, but undesirable, alternatives. They are (1) no animals have souls; (2) some have souls and others do not; (3) they all have souls. The first alternative is undesirable because, on the basis of the argument from analogy, there is *some ground* for believing that baboons and chimpanzees have souls; the second is undesirable because no boundary can be drawn between those animals who have souls from those who do not; and the third is undesirable, for it is highly improbable that oysters and sponges have souls. We have to choose which of the three alternatives is the least undesirable. The reasonable choice is the first alternative. This argument, which I have constructed from some of Descartes' remarks in his letters, has, in my opinion, some plausibility; but exactly what weight to assign to it, I do not know. There is simply no objective criterion by which an argument of this sort can be assigned its proper weight.

In presenting his doctrine that animals are pure automata, Descartes provided the foundations for a new materialism which was to challenge his philosophical position. If, as Descartes claims, these new materialists contend, that sensations and feelings can be replaced by brain events in conjunction with physiological mechanisms in providing adequate accounts of animal behavior, why should such a replacement stop with animals? Why not seek it for human beings as well? Thomas Huxley considered himself a disciple of Descartes when he wrote:

I am prepared to go with the materialists wherever the true pursuit of the *path of Descartes* may lead them. . . . I hold with the materialists, that the human body, like all living bodies, is a machine, all the operations of which, will sooner or later be explained on physical principles. I believe that we shall, sooner or later, arrive at a *mechanical equivalent of consciousness* just as we have arrived at a mechanical equivalent of heat.[22]

CHAPTER 11

The Physical World

DESCARTES' venture into skepticism enabled him to liberate himself from the common sense version of the nature of the physical world by suspending belief in the existence of the world. But, presently, having discovered that God exists, he is now in the position not only, so to speak, to bring back the world but also to reconstruct his conception of it along adequate scientific principles. The latter is the subject matter of the present chapter. The material for our discussion is not found in the *Meditations* but in *The World* and in the *Principles*. First, I shall treat the distinction Descartes made between such properties as figure, magnitude, motion, that is, *primary qualities*, and odor, color, sound, that is, *secondary qualities*. A clear statement of this distinction is found in one of Descartes' replies to the sixth set of objections:

> . . . I observed that nothing at all belonged to the nature or essence of body, except that it was a thing with length, breadth, and depth, admitting of various shapes and various motions. I found also that its shapes and motions were only modes, which no power could make to exist apart from it; and on the other hand that colours, odours, savours and the rest of such things, were merely sensations existing in my thought, and differing no less from bodies than pain differs from the shape and motion of the instrument which inflicts it. Finally, I saw that gravity, hardness, the power of heating, of attracting and of purging, and all other qualities which we experience in bodies, consisted solely in motion or its absence, and in the configuration and situation of their parts.[1]

What does Descartes mean by the last sentence in the above passage? Let us, in answering the question, consider "hardness," with the understanding that a somewhat similar analysis will

196

apply to the other members of the above list. According to Descartes, visible objects like chairs, sponges, and water are composed of imperceptible particles. Now, if two of them are in contact with each other but are not in motion relative to each other, some force, however small, is needed in order to separate them. And twice as much force is needed in order to move two of them as to move one; ten times to move ten of them, and so on. On the other hand, if two or more of these particles are in motion in different directions and touch each other, less force is needed to separate them than if they were not in motion; and no force if their own motion is sufficient to separate them. The above analysis is *the sole* basis for the difference between solid and fluid visible bodies.[2] The particles which compose a liquid are in constant motion and are easily separated from each other; whereas those of solids, being at rest relatively to one another, require force in order to be separated. Hardness for Descartes turns out to be, not a property of the fundamental particles of matter, but of wood, iron, and other visible solid objects. It is a property of these bodies, as he says, by virtue only "of the motion or its absence and in the configuration and situation" of the particles which compose them. The above analysis illustrates a fundamental principle which, together with his conception of matter as extension, constitutes Descartes' philosophy of nature, namely, "That all the variety in matter, or all the diversity of its forms, depends on motion."[3]

Descartes' statement "that colours, odours, savours, and the rest of such things were merely sensations existing in my thought" is somewhat misleading. He does not reject such propositions as "the shirt is blue" or "the fish has a foul odour"; what he insists, however, is that the term "blue" should not be taken to signify a property of the shirt which resembles the sensation a normal observer experiences when he sees a blue object under standard conditions. Insofar as color and smell are predicated of bodies, they are, according to Descartes, dispositional properties, namely, dispositions and capacities which bodies have of bringing about sensations of color and smell, under certain conditions, in human beings. In the *Principles*, Descartes says "... light, colours, smells, tastes, sounds and the tactile qualities ... are nothing more, as far as is known to us, than certain dispositions of objects consisting of magnitude, figure, and motion ..."4 "Colour," "odour," and "taste" are for Descartes Janus terms in that they serve a dual function: they refer to sensations in a man's soul, and in another, but related, sense, to the dispositions of a body by virtue of the magnitude and motion of its minute parts to bring about these sensations.

Descartes has two major arguments for the distinction between primary and secondary qualities. The first is as follows:

> We have only to attend to our idea of some body, e.g., a stone and remove from it whatever we know is not entailed by the very nature of body. In the first place, then, we may reject hardness, because if the stone were liquified or reduced to powder, it would no longer possess hardness, and yet would not cease to be a body; let us in the next place reject colour, because we have often seen stones so transparent that they had no colour; again we reject weight, because we see that fire although very light is yet body.... After examination we shall find that there is nothing remaining in the idea of body excepting that it is extended in length, breadth and depth.[5]

This argument is not, in my opinion, a strong one; for Descartes has only shown that each secondary quality is dispensable for something's being a body, but not that they are dispensable as a group. This latter criticism might be held to be due to a misunderstanding of Descartes' argument, since in the first sentence of the above passage Descartes speaks of those properties which are not "entailed by the very nature of body." Descartes is claiming that he clearly and distinctly perceives that nothing is essential for the nature of body except that it occupy space in length, breadth, and depth, and that, consequently, secondary qualities collectively are not essential for something's being a body. Descartes' observation that certain stones are colorless and that fire has no weight is not required in his argument and was used merely to illustrate his *a priori* claim. But this new interpretation fares no better than the previous one. In the eighteenth century, George Berkley held that he could not conceive a body to exist without at least some secondary qualities. How are we to decide in this matter between Descartes and Berkley? We cannot, since, as indicated previously, Descartes proposed no criterion by which we can determine whether a specified set of properties is sufficient to characterize the nature of body.

Descartes, in the above argument, assumes that all properties of a body necessarily belong to it. Thus, he rules out color as a nondispositional property on the ground that transparent stones are not colored. The Scholastics called properties which are not essential to the existence of a body, but which, nevertheless belong to it, accidents. One question, then, is why did Descartes rule out the existence of accidents? He gave two reasons. The first is that a person who claims that there are accidents is confusing the ideas of mode and substance. "... It is contradictory," he writes, "that real accidents should exist, because whatever is real can exist separately apart from any other subject; but whatever can exist separately is substance, not accident."[6] This criticism of the Scholastics, who accepted the existence of accidents, is a straw man argument, since by "a real accident" they did not mean something which "can exist separately apart from any other subject" but rather a mode of a substance which the substance does not necessarily require in order to exist. Descartes' second reason is that the idea of a body with accidents is not a clear and distinct one. An idea is clear and distinct, according to Descartes (and as we discussed in the second chapter), when the elements of which the idea is composed are necessarily connected so that one can make logical inferences from one to the other. Now obviously, since accidents are neither part of the essence of a body nor necessarily connected with it, the idea of a body with accidents cannot be clear and distinct in Descartes' sense of the term.

Descartes' second argument for the distinction between primary and secondary qualities is that secondary qualities as (nondispositional) properties of bodies are not needed for the purpose of explaining natural phenomena:

I recognize no kind of matter in corporeal objects except that matter susceptible of every sort of division, shape, and motion which geometers call quantity and which they presuppose as the subject matter of their proofs. Further the only properties I consider in it are those divisions, shapes and motions; and about them I accept only what can be derived from indubitably true axioms with the sort of self-evidence which belongs to a mathematical proof. All natural phenomena, as I shall show, can be explained in this way. I therefore do not think any other principles in physics are either necessary or desirable.[7]

In the above passage, Descartes says that shape, magnitude, and motion are the only properties that are needed in order to give an adequate account for natural phenomena; and by implication he is denying that color, sound, and smell are needed. The importance of the above passage is in Descartes' contention that primary qualities can account for *all phenomena*. It is not, after all, very surprising that explanatory theories, by referring only to primary qualities, can adequately explain the behavior of projectiles or the movement of planets. What is central to Descartes' argument is that such theories can also account for our experiences of seemingly qualitative states such as the changing color of leaves in autumn and the foul odor emanating from rotting fish. Descartes' mechanism is geometrical, since the only properties other than motion that are involved in his account of natural phenomena are geometrical ones. Thus, for instance, Descartes attributes our experiences of heat and light to the violent movements of minute unobserved particles and the difference in our qualitative experiences of them to differences in the sizes and shapes of the particles involved. This is, in my opinion, a formidable argument for rejecting the position that heat, color, smell, and sound are nondispositional properties of bodies. I do not say this because Descartes' theory of nature is a correct one—a part of it was in fact discarded for good scientific reasons—but because he was right in principle, for he correctly discerned the direction which the new emerging mathematical physics was to take. We are to think of bodies as consisting of unobservable particles which have no secondary qualities and which behave in accordance with a few mechanical principles. This theoretical model is then to be used for the purpose of explaining the rich variety of things, states, and processes which we experience by our senses.

I   *Two Objections to Descartes' Theory of Matter*

Descartes, as we have seen, considered extension to be the essence of matter. While he was certain of this fact because he believed that he clearly and distinctly perceived it to be true, he nevertheless realized that his position was exposed to a number of objections which he had to meet: "The first is that prevalent opinion that most bodies are capable of being rarefied and condensed; so that when rarefied they have greater extension than when condensed; and some have even subtilized to such an extent that they desire to distinguish the substance of a body from its quantity, and its quantity from its extension."[8] When a piece of iron is rarefied it spreads out over a larger area of space, and, while the quantity of matter remains constant throughout the process, the extension has increased. It follows then, contrary to Descartes' position, that matter cannot be identified with extension.

The assumption in the above criticism, which is false according to Descartes, is that the volume of space encompassed by the extremities of a dense body contains the same amount of matter as it does when rarefied. Consider a sponge, says Descartes, whose pores are first filled with water and then compressed and dried. The extremities of the sponge encompass a larger area of space in the former instance than in the latter; but since the pores are no part of the matter of the sponge, the sponge itself occupies the same amount of space as previously. What accounts for the difference in the volume of space encompassed by the extremities in the two instances is the difference in the quantity of matter involved. In the former, it was the matter of the sponge and the water; in the latter instance the water was eliminated. The sponge illustration provided Descartes with the basis for his approach to rarefied and condensed bodies; rarefied bodies, being more porous than condensed ones, are filled in their interstices with minute unobservable particles like water in the pores of a sponge.[9]

The second objection to Descartes' theory of matter is that he has failed to distinguish body from space. Descartes raises this objection against his own position: "The second reason is that when we conceive that there is extension in length, breadth and depth only, we are not in the habit of saying that there is a body, but only space and further empty space, which most people persuade themselves is a mere negation."[10]

In order to meet this criticism, Descartes first tries to show how space and body are to be distinguished within the framework of his theory. He frankly admits that there is no real distinction between them but only a distinction of reason: "Space or internal place and the corporeal substance which is contained in it, are not different otherwise than in the mode in which they are conceived by us. For, in truth, the same extension in length, breadth and depth, which constitutes space, constitutes body..."[11] Gottlob Frege's distinction between meaning and reference might be useful in the present context. When I point to some X and say, "This body," or point to it and say, "This area of space," I am referring to the identical bit of extension in both cases. But in my using the term "body" in the first instance, I am ignoring X's position relative to other bodies in its vicinity, and simply mean by the term the figure and magnitude which is true of X. On the other hand, when in the second instance I use the term "space," I ignore the kind of body X is, and simply mean by the term the position of this body relative to other bodies in its vicinity. The above analysis, I believe, provides us with the clue for understanding the following remark by Descartes: "... the same extension which constitutes the nature of body likewise constitutes the nature of space, nor do the two mutually differ, excepting as the nature of the genus or species differs from the nature of the individual...."[12]

There is a difference between identifying the extension as bodily and as spatial. In the former case, we think of extension as individuated in this or that particular body; it is the extension of this stone or that lizard. Thus, as the body changes its position (motion) relative to other bodies in its vicinity, the position of the extension has changed as well. On the other hand, when we conceive extension spatially, we do not consider it individuated but rather indeterminate with respect to any particular body. Consequently, when body X changes its position relative to other bodies in its vicinity and another body Y of the same figure and magnitude occupies its position, the spatial extension which first characterized X now characterizes Y.

Descartes' theory of matter, however, given the above analysis of space *seems* to be exposed to a strong objection. Suppose a tube was emptied of its contents and absolutely nothing remained within the tube; in other words, there was a vacuum within it. On Descartes' theory of space, I can still refer to the space within the tube. I would be referring to the position of the figure and magnitude of the cavity within the tube relative to the tube and to the other bodies surrounding it. But then, on Descartes' theory that the essence of matter is extension and that there are no accidental properties, there can be no distinction between the vacuum and the body, for the former is extended in length, breadth, and depth in the same way as is the body.

The above criticism requires the assumption that a vacuum is possible. Consequently, in order to safeguard his position, Descartes not only rejects the existence of a vacuum but the very possibility of its existence. He writes: "And therefore, if it is asked what would happen if God removed all the body contained in a vessel without permitting its place being occupied by another body, we shall answer that the sides of the vessel will thereby come into immediate contiguity with one another. For two bodies must touch when there is nothing between them. . . ."[13] The impossibility of a vacuum is entailed by Descartes' conception of extension as the essence of body; hence, to argue that Descartes failed to distinguish a vacuum from a body is simply to beg the point at issue.

II *Descartes' Theory of Motion*

In Part 2 of the *Principles*, Descartes characterizes motion as "the transportation of one part of matter or one body from the vicinity of those bodies that are in immediate contact with it, and which we regard as in repose, into the vicinity of others." He adds that by using the term "transportation" in the above definition, he intends to signify that motion should be understood as change from one position to another and not the force or action which is required for the movement to occur.

And his final point is that motion is not a substance but only a mode of the thing moved in the same sense, as figure is a mode of the figured thing.[14]

Descartes' theory of motion is clearly a relativist one. A body when considered by itself cannot meaningfully be said to be at rest or in motion. Moreover, if the distance between two bodies is increasing, and there is no third body to which we can relate them, it makes no difference whether we say that both bodies are in motion or that one is in motion and the other at rest. The only thing we can possibly mean, according to Descartes, when we speak of a body at rest or in motion is that the body is in a certain position relative to the bodies it is in immediate contact with; if it has passed from the vicinity of one set of bodies to another, it has moved; if not, it is at rest. Thus, we say that the passenger is at rest in the moving ship, despite the fact that the position of his body relative to the shore is changing, because his position relative to the bodies in his *immediate* vicinity, namely, the parts of the ship, has not changed.

Henry More in a letter to Descartes raised two objections to Descartes' theory of motion. Descartes had in the *Principles* denied that motion is due to some agency within a body, such as impetus, force, or energy; but, says More, unless there was some dynamical principle in matter, "motion, being so feeble and evanescent," would at once cease throughout all of nature. More's point is that motion is not a geometrical property like figure or volume, and thus it cannot be accounted for by extension. The only sources for motion are dynamical properties, which Descartes rejects as properties of matter.

To More's criticism Descartes answers: "I agree that *if matter is left to itself and receives no impulse from anywhere it will remain entirely still.* But it receives an impulse from God who preserves the same amount of motion or translation in it as He placed in it at the beginning."[15] Descartes' answer seems to be either an evasion of the criticism or a paradoxical response to it. It is the former, if Descartes is merely claiming that God, in creating the world, introduced a certain quantity of motion within it and conserves the latter from moment to moment. Let us spell out this point. According to Descartes, it is conceivable that God could have created matter without motion; hence extension and motion are distinct acts of creation. God created matter, continuous and without limit, and introduced motion into the extended world body, and thus brought into being a plurality of bodies. The fundamental difference between extension and motion is that the former is the essence of matter; motion is not. I can conceive the world as an extended body without motion but I cannot conceive motion except as a mode of an extended body. Now, in introducing motion in the extended body, God, being constant and changeless, maintains in the physical world the same total amount of motion which he placed into it on the first day of creation: "For although movement is no more than a mode of this matter which is moved, there is yet a certain determinate quantity of it which never increases or diminishes though in certain of the parts of matter there is sometimes more of it and sometimes less."[16] The above account is an evasion of More's criticism, because More, like Descartes, being a devout Christian, had no doubt that God was *the first cause* of motion. What puzzled him in Descartes' account of motion is that by eliminating dynamical properties, such as force and energy from bodies, Descartes had also eliminated *the secondary causes* which could possibly account for motion, that is, the mechanism by which God sustains the same quantity of motion in the world. Descartes would not have evaded More's criticism had he meant that God is the direct cause of motion in that His activity is the dynamical principle which, without any intervening causes, brings about the motion of each and every body in the universe. This position when spelled out, however, is paradoxical. It signifies that God *alone* causes one billiard ball to move toward another which is at rest and, on the occasion of the impact between them, causes the other billiard ball to move.

More's second criticism consists in challenging Descartes' claim that motion, like figure, is a mode of a body. We observe, says More, bodies transferring their motions to other bodies; but if motion, like figure, is a mode of a body, how could it, any more than figure, leave one body and enter another? Descartes' response is as follows: "You observe correctly that *a motion, being a mode of a body cannot pass from one body to another*. But that is not what I wrote; indeed I think that motion, considered as such a mode, continually changes."[17] More failed to appreciate Descartes' relational account of motion. For Descartes, motion, unlike figure, is a relational mode of a body in the same sense as being short is a relational property of a man. A man is short by virtue of his height relative to the height of other men; and a body has the property of rest or motion by virtue of its location relative to the bodies in its immediate vicinity. On the other hand, a body has a determinate figure irrespective of what might be true of other bodies. Notice that in the above quotation, Descartes denies, despite the loose way in which he often writes on this subject, that there is a transference of motion from one body to another. True, his third law of nature states that when two or more bodies encounter each other, each loses no more movement than is acquired by the other; but he does not say that there is a transference of motion from one to the other. On a purely relational theory of motion like Descartes', the only thing that transference of motion from one body to another could possibly mean is that the loss of motion of one body is the occasion, but not the cause, for the acquisition of motion by the other body. Descartes never drew this occasionalist conclusion, but I cannot see how, given his theory of motion, he could evade it.

III   *The Laws of Nature*

Descartes, in *The World*, claimed that the laws of nature, which are employed in presently explaining the orderly occurrences of events in nature, can also be used to account for the present order in the world. Let us imagine, he said, a world very much like our own and that God created its matter and divided it into many parts, some greater, some smaller, some of one figure, others of another:

. . . let us [further] suppose that the only distinction to be met with consists in the variety of the motions He gives to them, in causing that, at the very instant that they are created, some of them begin to move in one direction, others in another; some more swiftly, others more slowly (or, if you please, not at all), and that they continue thereafter their motions according to the ordinary laws of nature; for God has so marvellously ordained these laws that, although we should suppose that He had created nothing more than what I have said, and even that He had established therein no order or proportion, but that He had made a chaos the most confused and the most perplexed that poets could describe, they would be sufficient to cause the parts of this chaos to disentangle themselves, and to arrange themselves in such good order that they would take the form of a very perfect world, and one in which not only light would be seen, but also all other things, in general and particular, which appear in this real world.[18]

In referring to the laws of nature in the above passage as "ordained" by God, Descartes clearly implies that there is nothing about the nature of matter which could account for the fact that bodies behave in accordance with laws. Notice also that Descartes distinguishes between a lawlike world and an orderly one; for he claims above that even if the world on the first moment of creation was a chaos, the laws of nature having been decreed by God would be sufficient to transform it into an orderly cosmos. By the latter I think he was referring to those facts about the world which have impressed philosophers, from Plato to the present, as constituting evidence of design and purpose in nature, for example, that the planets move in uniform orbits around a given point and that bees seem to behave as if they were conscious of goals and adopted means for achieving them. Descartes obviously could not deny such facts; but he insisted that, in order to account for them, we have no need to postulate purposes and goals in nature. These *seeming* final causes can be fully accounted for by matter behaving in accordance with the laws of nature.

Descartes lists three primary laws of nature, which he calls "principles"; and from them he deduces seven "general rules." Let us consider the three primary laws. The first is: "... That each thing as far as in it lies continues always in the same state; and that which is once moved always continues so to move."[19] This law specifies what happens to a body when it is not being acted upon by other bodies; if it has a certain magnitude, it will maintain the same magnitude; if at rest, it will remain at rest; and if in motion, it will continue to move with unaltered velocity. What is contrary to the prevalent opinion

in Descartes' time is the last item. It was held, following
Aristotle, that all motion requires a mover; whereas, according
to the above principle, it is only change of motion which requires one. In defending his own position and criticizing the
followers of Aristotle, Descartes asks why a principle of inertia
should apply to a body respecting its magnitude, figure, and
state of rest but not toward its motion? An immutable God
who always acts in the same way would surely not permit
motion to be an exception to the general rule.[20] Moreover,
Aristotle's principle that all motion requires a mover cannot
provide a reason why a stone continues to move after it has
left the hand of the person who threw it. According to Descartes,
it is not that it continues to be in motion that requires an
explanation, but the fact that it does not continue to move
forever. The reason for this latter fact, according to Descartes, is
that the air in which the body is moving offers it resistance.[21]

The second law of nature is that all bodies in motion tend
to move in a straight line.[22] What has to be stressed is that this
law refers to the "inclination to move" and not to actual motion.
For, according to Descartes, since there is no void and all
places are filled with bodies, the only movement is circular
and vortical; when one body leaves its place it enters the place
of another body, and this other body the place of a third, and
so on, the last body occupies at the same instant the place
left by the first body. The whole process, in order to preclude
the possibility of a void, has to take place simultaneously.
Descartes insists that there is no inconsistency between his
vortical conception of motion and his second law. Each part
of matter, while moving circularly as the result of the impact
on it of other bodies, nevertheless has a tendency at each
instant to move in a straight line. Descartes illustrates his meaning with an example which also provides evidence for the
second law. If a stone is whirled in a sling, the stone presses
upon the center of the sling and stretches the chord. This
indicates that the stone has a tendency to move in a straight
line, and that it moves in a circle only because it is forced
to do so.[23]

I referred to the third law previously in discussing Descartes'
reply to More. That law states that when bodies encounter each

other, each body loses no more movement than is acquired by the others. Descartes contends that it is due to this law that the total movement in the world remains the same throughout its existence. What should be stressed, in referring to Descartes' laws of nature, is that he tries to derive them from the fact that nature was created and is sustained in existence by a God who is immutable and constant in his ways; thus, we can have assurance that nature is uniform and economical. The reason, for instance, that God adopted motion in a straight line as natural to bodies is because this type of motion is the simplest. The fact, however, that the fundamental principles of physics are grounded on metaphysics does not stop Descartes from also employing, as we have seen, empirical arguments for his laws, and from claiming that his principles can offer the best accounting of what we observe with our senses.

Despite Descartes' ingenuity in presenting his three laws of nature, it seems to me that they are inconsistent with his claim that the only primary qualities of bodies are geometrical ones plus motion. Laws of nature are not causal agencies; they merely describe what is constant and unvarying in nature. Descartes' first law does not cause a body which is in motion to continue moving; what causes it to do so is that it has, according to the first law, a natural tendency to behave this way. But how could bodies have tendencies to rest, or to move in straight lines, or to gain or to lose motion when encountering other bodies, when their only properties, besides motion, are geometrical ones? They surely could not have these tendencies by virtue of their geometrical properties; nor could they have it by virtue of the fact that they are capable of motion, for their capability does not dictate that they would have a tendency to move in a straight line or to continue to move when in motion. I think it is inescapable that Descartes cannot consistently maintain both his geometrical conception of matter and his three laws of nature.

IV   *Cosmogony*

Given the three primary laws of nature, how, according to Descartes, could an orderly cosmos have emerged from the original state of chaos? He begins by describing how what he calls "the second element" came into being. When God first introduced motion into the material world, the parts of matter which were moved had at the start every conceivable shape and size with several angles and sides like the pieces which split off from a stone when it is broken:

... it is certain that afterward, in moving and striking against one another, they would have rubbed off, little by little, the small points of their angles, and blunted the edges of their sides until they become by degrees almost all round, as grains of sand and flint do when rolled about in running water; so that there might not now be any noticeable difference between those which are near enough together, nor even between those which are very distant, except in the fact that they can move a little faster, and be a little smaller or larger, one than the other; and this does not prevent our attributing to all of them the same form.[24]

Almost all of matter consists of these very minute nonvisible spherical particles of the second element. There are, however, two exceptions which constitute the two other elements. There are those parts of matter which at the start, being much larger and slower in motion than the others, have not been divided or rounded as easily as the others; and consequently, since they possess very irregular and resistant shapes, have tended to unite in a mass rather than be ground up and become round. These parts of matter constitute the third element which compose the planets and the comets. The second exception is the matter which has come off from the surface of the parts of the second element in proportion as they grind each other to ever smaller bodies. These ground-off bits of matter form the first element which Descartes describes as a "virtually perfect fluid" and which fill all interstices no matter how small.

Now, however chaotic the movements which God has permitted matter on first creating it, the parts of matter, in pushing against one another, must eventually reach a degree of adjustment. This takes the form of gigantic vortices in which the three elements come into being and occupy positions appropriate to their sizes and motions. Descartes claims that, on the basis of his three laws of nature and the general rules derived from them, it can be shown that the first element, besides occupying interstices between the bodies of the second and third elements, will also assemble at the center of each vortex, thus forming the sun and all the other stars. He also maintains that the second element, consisting of the very minute small round particles, will occupy the rest of each vortex, with the exception of bodies like the earth and the comets which constitute the third element. What should be noted here is that what most people think of as the vast empty spaces between the stars is for Descartes a plenum filled with the invisible particles of the second element.

Descartes' cosmogony, as his physics, in general, is today of mere historical interest, for it is Newtonian and not Cartesian physics which is to be found in standard physics texts. On the other hand, Descartes' metaphysics, particularly his conception of man as an intimate union of body and mind, and his theory of innate ideas, are regarded in present philosophical circles as possible candidates for the truth. The evidence for the latter is that Descartes' position on these matters is both defended and criticized in contemporary journals.

Notes and References

Whenever possible I have referred the reader to English translations of Descartes' works. When I thought, however, that clarity would be gained in altering the translation, while still adhering to the original text, I did not hesitate to do so.

Chapter One

1. *The Philosophical Works of Descartes*, trans. Elizabeth S. Haldane and G. R. T. Ross, 2 vols. (Cambridge: Cambridge University Press, 1967), I, 85; hereafter cited as *HR*.
2. *HR*, I, 85–86.
3. Ibid., 119.
4. Ibid., 86.
5. Ibid., 87.
6. Quoted from Norman Kemp Smith, *New Studies in the Philosophy of Descartes* (London: Macmillan, 1952), p. 11 (did not use his brackets). Also in *HR*, I, 87.
7. *Oeuvres de Descartes*, ed. Charles Adam and Paul Tannery, 13 vols. (Paris: Cerf, 1897–1913), X, 52; hereafter cited as *AT*.
8. *HR*, I, 13.
9. Ibid., 92.
10. The references to Descartes' life including the above narrative about his dreams are to be found in Adrien Baillet's *La Vie de Monsieur Descartes* (Paris, 1691).
11. Op. cit., Smith, p. 11. Also in *HR*, I, 87.
12. *AT*, V, 133. Also, Émile Bréhier, *The History of Philosophy*, IV (Chicago: The University of Chicago Press, 1938), 51–52.
13. *HR*, I, 133.
14. Émile Boutroux, *Historical Studies in Philosophy* (London: Macmillan, 1912), p. 238.
15. From the opening paragraph of Arthur Schopenhauer's *Sketch of a History of the Doctrine of the Ideal and Real. Philosophy of Arthur Schopenhauer* (New York: Tudor Publishing Co., 1936), p. 101. Translated by Belfort Bax and Bailey Saunders.

Chapter Two

1. *HR*, I, 3.
2. Ibid.

3. Ibid., 3–4; italics mine.

4. Ibid., 5.

5. Ibid.

6. Ibid., 28.

7. Richard McKeon, trans., *The Basic Works of Aristotle* (New York: Random House, 1941), p. 936.

8. *HR*, I, 1.

9. Ibid.

10. Ibid., 2.

11. Ibid., 211.

12. Ibid., 7.

13. Ibid.

14. Ibid.

15. Op. cit., Smith, p. 71.

16. *HR*, I, 8.

17. *AT*, IX, 205.

18. *HR*, II, 152.

19. Ibid., 214.

20. *HR*, I, 26.

21. Ibid., 9.

22. For a discussion on this issue see Alan Gewirth, "Clearness and Distinctness in Descartes," *Philosophy* 18 (April, 1943), 17–36.

23. *HR*, I, 92.

24. Ibid., 30.

25. Ibid., 92.

26. Ibid.

27. Ibid., 14.

28. Ibid., 23–24.

29. Ibid., 47.

30. Ibid., 40–41.

31. Ibid., 41–42.

32. Ibid., 42.

33. Ibid., 43.

34. L. J. Beck, *The Method of Descartes: A Study of the "Regulae"* (Oxford: Oxford University Press, Clarendon Press, 1952), p. 78.

35. *HR*, I, 34.

36. Anthony Kenny, *Descartes* (New York: Random House, 1968), p. 99.

37. *HR*, II, 67–68.

38. *Descartes' Philosophical Letters*, trans. and ed. Anthony Kenny (Oxford: Oxford University Press, Clarendon Press), p. 123; hereafter cited as *PL*.

39. *HR*, I, 237.

40. Ibid.

41. Ibid., 153–54

42. Ibid., 264.

43. See the article by Gewirth.

44. *HR*, I, 39.

45. *AT*, II, 598.

46. *HR*, I, 157.

47. *HR*, II, 49–50.

48. *HR*, I, 56.

49. See Robert McRae, "Innate Ideas," in *Cartesian Studies*, ed. R. J. Butler (New York: Barnes & Noble, 1972), pp. 32–54.

50. James Collins, *Descartes' "Philosophy of Nature*," American Philosophical Quarterly Monograph Series (Oxford, 1971), p. 60.

51. Op. cit., Smith, p. 99 (did not use his brackets). Also in *HR*, I, 121.

52. *PL*, p. 197.

53. *HR*, I, 59–61.

54. Ibid., 60.

Chapter Three

1. *HR*, I, 144.

2. Harry G. Frankfurt, *Deamons, Dreamers, and Madmen* (Indianapolis: Bobbs-Merrill, 1970), pp. 4–5.

3. *AT*, VII, 156.

4. *HR*, II, 282.

5. *HR*, I, 250.

6. Ibid., 237.

7. *HR*, II, 60.

8. Ibid., 49–50.

9. *HR*, I, 140; italics mine.

10. Ibid., 145.

11. *HR*, II, 60–61.

12. *HR*, I, 145.

13. Ibid.

14. Ibid.

15. Ibid., 145–46; italics mine.

16. Ibid., 146.

17. Ibid., 314; italics mine.

18. Ibid., 101; italics mine.

19. Ibid, 146.

20. Ibid.

21. Ibid., 147.
22. Ibid.
23. Ibid.
24. Ibid.
25. Ibid.
26. Ibid.
27. Ibid., 148.
28. Ibid.
29. Ibid.

Chapter Four

1. *HR*, I, 149.
2. Ibid., 101.
3. Ibid., 150; italics mine.
4. Ibid., 153.
5. *HR*, II, 38.
6. Ibid., 207.
7. *HR*, I, 240.
8. David Hume, *A Treatise of Human Nature* (Oxford: Oxford University Press, Clarendon Press, 1888), p. 252.
9. Ibid., p. 253.
10. A. Boyce Gibson, *The Philosophy of Descartes* (New York: Russell & Russell, 1967), p. 85.
11. S. V. Keeling, *Descartes* (London: Oxford University Press, 1968), p. 99.
12. *HR*, II, 42.
13. *HR*, I, 158–59.
14. Ibid., 150.
15. Ibid.
16. Ibid., 324.
17. *HR*, II, 49–50.
18. *HR*, I, 151; italics mine.
19. Ibid., 151–52.
20. Robert McRae, "Descartes' Definition of Thought," in *Cartesian Studies*, ed. R. J. Butler (New York: Barnes & Noble, 1972), pp. 56–57.
21. *HR*, I, 153.
22. Ibid., 319; italics mine.
23. Ibid., 152.
24. *PL*, p. 87.
25. *HR*, I, 239.
26. Ibid., 240.

27. *AT*, V, 154.
28. *HR*, I, 245–46.
29. *Ibid.*, 151.
30. Ibid., 151–53.
31. *HR*, II, 101.
32. *HR*, I, 153–54.
33. Ibid., 154.
34. Ibid.
35. Ibid., 154–55.
36. Ibid., 155–56.
37. Ibid., 157.

Chapter Five

1. *HR*, I, 158.
2. Benedict De Spinoza, *Ethics of Benedict De Spinoza*, Prop. XLIII. Translated by W. Hale White; revised by Amelia Hutchison. (London: Oxford University Press, 1910, 4th ed.), p. 89.
3. *HR*, I, 158–59; italics mine.
4. Alan Gewirth, "The Cartesian Circle," *The Philosophical Review* 50 (July, 1941).
5. Harry Frankfurt, "Descartes' Validation of Reason," *American Philosophical Quarterly* 2, no. 2 (April, 1965).
6. *HR*, II, 39.
7. *HR*, I, 183–84; italics mine.
8. *HR*, II, 92.
9. Ibid., 38.
10. Ibid., 115; italics mine.

Chapter Six

1. *HR*, I, 159.
2. Ibid., 160.
3. *PL*, p. 104.
4. *HR*, I, 160.
5. Ibid.
6. Ibid., 161.
7. Ibid., 442.
8. *PL*, p. 111.
9. Op. cit., Kenny, p. 100. Also in *PL*, p. 117.
10. *HR*, I, 165.
11. Ibid., 161–62.
12. *HR*, II, 71.
13. Ibid., 2.
14. *HR*, I, 162.

15. Ibid., 162–63.
16. *HR*, II, 10–11.
17. See Kenny, pp. 126–45.
18. *HR*, I, 163.
19. Ibid., 164.
20. Ibid., 165; italics mine.
21. *AT*, V, 152. Also cited in Kenny, p. 118.
22. *HR*, I, 166.
23. Ibid.
24. Ibid.
25. *HR*, II, 218. See Descartes' reply to Gassendi's criticism.
26. *PL*, p. 147.
27. *HR*, I, 167.
28. Ibid., 168.
29. Ibid.
30. Ibid.
31. Ibid., 169.
32. Ibid.
33. Ibid.
34. Ibid., 170.
35. Ibid.

Chapter Seven

1. *HR*, I, 179–80.
2. *HR*, II, 20.
3. *HR*, I, 104.
4. Ibid., 180–81.
5. Ibid., 182.
6. *AT*, VII, 323. Also in *HR*, II, 186.
7. *HR*, II, 228.
8. Ibid., 21; italics mine.
9. St. Thomas Aquinas, *Truth*, trans. Robert W. Mulligan (Chicago: Henry Regnery Co., 1952), I, 141.
10. *PL*, pp. 14–15.
11. Ibid., p. 236.
12. *HR*, II, 248.
13. *AT*, IV, 118.
14. *PL*, p. 241.
15. Anton C. Pegis, *Basic Writings of St. Thomas Aquinas* (New York: Random House, 1944), I, 265.
16. *AT*, I, 149.
17. *AT*, IV, 118.

Chapter Eight

1. *HR*, I, 232.
2. Ibid., 174.
3. Ibid., 175; italics mine.
4. Ibid., 175–76.
5. Ibid., 176.
6. Ibid., 177.
7. Ibid., 185.
8. Ibid., 186.
9. Ibid.
10. Ibid.
11. *PL*, p. 76.
12. *HR*, I, 186–87.
13. Ibid., 189–90.
14. Ibid., 191.
15. Ibid.
16. Ibid.
17. Ibid.
18. Ibid., 188.
19. Ibid., 192.
20. Ibid., 193.
21. Ibid.
22. Ibid., 194–98.
23. Ibid., 198–99.

Chapter Nine

1. *PL*, p. 52.
2. *HR*, I, 190.
3. Ibid., 244.
4. Ibid., p. 243.
5. *HR*, II, 83.
6. Ibid., 98.
7. Ibid., 100.
8. Kenny, p. 95.
9. *HR*, I, 196.
10. *HR*, II, 99.
11. *HR*, I, 192.
12. Ibid., 193–94.
13. *HR*, II, 99.
14. *PL*, p. 51.
15. Smith, p. 147.
16. *AT*, VI, 113.

Chapter Ten

1. Kenny, pp. 222–23; italics mine.
2. *PL*, p. 138.
3. Ibid., p. 138.
4. Ibid., p. 141.
5. Ibid.
6. *HR*, I, 347.
7. Ibid.; the term "animal spirits" does not signify anything spiritual. The animal spirits are small particles which are conducted into the nerves and muscles whereby they move the body in diverse ways.
8. Ibid., 346.
9. *PL*, p. 206.
10. *HR*, II, 104.
11. *HR*, I, 116.
12. Ibid.
13. Keith Gunderson, "Descartes, La Mettrie, Language and Machines," *Philosophy* 39 (July, 1964).
14. *PL*, p. 245.
15. *HR*, I, 116.
16. Zeno Vendler, *Res Cogitans* (Ithaca: Cornell University Press, 1972), p. 155.
17. *HR*, I, 192.
18. *PL*, p. 243.
19. Ibid.
20. Ibid., p. 244.
21. Ibid., p. 208.
22. Quoted from introduction to *Descartes Selections*, trans. and ed. Ralph M. Eaton (New York: Scribner's, 1955), p. xxvi; italics mine; hereafter cited as *DS*.

Chapter Eleven

1. *HR*, II, 253–54.
2. *AT*, XI, 10–13.
3. *HR*, I, 265.
4. Ibid., 296.
5. *AT*, VIII, 65. Also in *HR*, I, 259.
6. *HR*, II, 250.
7. *AT*, VIII, 78. Also cited in Kenny, pp. 203–204.
8. *HR*, I, 256.
9. Ibid., 256–57.
10. Ibid., 256.

11. Ibid., 259.
12. Ibid.
13. Ibid., 263.
14. Ibid., 266.
15. *PL*, p 258.
16. *AT*, IX, 83–84.
17. *PL*, 258.
18. *DS*, p. 320.
19. *HR*, I, 267.
20. *DS*, pp. 323–24.
21. Ibid., p. 325.
22. *HR*, I, 267.
23. *DS*, p. 327.
24. Ibid., p. 332.

Selected Bibliography

PRIMARY SOURCES

Oeuvres de Descartes. Edited by Charles Adam and Paul Tannery. 13 vols. Paris: Cerf, 1897–1913.

Descartes: Correspondence. Edited by Charles Adam and Gerard Milhaud. 8 vols. Paris: Félix Alcan, Presses Universitaires de France, 1936–1963.

The Philosophical Works of Descartes. Translated by Elizabeth S. Haldane and G. R. T. Ross. 2 vols. Cambridge: Cambridge University Press, 1967.

Descartes' Philosophical Writings. Translated by Norman Kemp Smith. London: Macmillan, 1952.

Descartes' Philosophical Letters. Translated and edited by Anthony Kenny. Oxford: Oxford University Press, Clarendon Press, 1970.

Descartes: Selections. Translated and edited by Ralph M. Eaton. New York: Scribner's, 1955.

SECONDARY SOURCES

1. Books

BALZ, ALBERT G. A. *Descartes and the Modern Mind.* New Haven: Yale University Press, 1952.

BECK, L. J. *The Metaphysics of Descartes.* Oxford: Oxford University Press, Clarendon Press, 1965.

—————. *The Method of Descartes.* Oxford: Oxford University Press, Clarendon Press, 1952.

FRANKFURT, HARRY G. *Deamons, Dreamers, and Madmen.* Indianapolis: Bobbs-Merrill, 1970.

GIBSON, A. BOYCE. *The Philosophy of Descartes.* 1932. Reprint. New York: Russell and Russell, 1967.

GOUHIER, HENRI. *La Pensée Metaphysique de Descartes.* Paris: J. Vrin, 1962.

JOACHIM, HAROLD H. *Descartes' Rules for the Direction of the Mind.* London: George Allen & Unwin, 1957.

KEELING, S. V. *Descartes.* London: Oxford University Press, 1968.

KENNY, ANTHONY. *Descartes.* New York: Random House, 1968.

PRICHARD, H. A. *Knowledge and Perception.* Oxford: Oxford University Press, Clarendon Press, 1950.

LAPORTE, JEAN. *Le Rationalisme de Descartes.* 2nd ed. Paris: Presses Universitaires de France, 1950.

ROTH, LEON. *Descartes' Discourse on Method.* Oxford: Oxford University Press, Clarendon Press, 1937.

SMITH, NORMAN KEMP. *New Studies in the Philosophy of Descartes.* London: Macmillan, 1952.

VERSFELD, MARTHINUS. *An Essay on The Metaphysics of Descartes.* London: Methuen, 1940.

2. Articles

AYER, A. J. "*Cogito, Ergo Sum.*" *Analysis* 14, no. 2 (December, 1953), pp. 27–31.

BOUWSMA, O. K. "DesCartes' Skepticism of the Senses." *Mind* 54 (October, 1945), pp. 313–32.

CHAPPELL, V. C. "The Concept of Dreaming." *Philosophical Quarterly* 13 (July, 1963), pp. 193–213.

DONEY, WILLIS. "The Cartesian Circle." *Journal of the History of Ideas* 16, no. 3 (June, 1955), pp. 324–38.

FRANKFURT, HARRY G. "Descartes Validation of Reason." *American Philosophical Quarterly* 2, no. 2 (April, 1965), pp. 149–56.

––––––. "Memory and the Cartesian Circle." *Philosophical Review* 71, no. 4 (October, 1962), pp. 504–11.

GEWIRTH, ALAN. "The Cartesian Circle." *Philosophical Review* 50, no. 4 (July, 1941), pp. 368–95.

GUNDERSON, KEITH. "Descartes, La Mettrie, Language and Machines." *Philosophy* 39 (July, 1964), pp. 193–222.

HARTLAND-SWANN, JOHN. "Descartes' Simple Natures." *Philosophy* 22 (July, 1947), pp. 139–52.

HINTIKKA, JAAKKO. "*Cogito, Ergo Sum*: Inference or Performance?" *Philosophical Review* 71, no. 1 (January, 1962), pp. 3–32.

MALCOM, NORMAN. "Descartes' Proof That His Essence is Thinking." *Philosophical Review* 74, no. 3 (July, 1965), pp. 315–38.

MILLER, LEONARD. "Descartes, Mathematics and God." *Philosophical Review* 66, no. 4 (October, 1957), pp. 451–65.

NASON, JOHN W. "Leibnitz's Attack on the Cartesian Doctrine of Extension." *Journal of The History of Ideas* 7, no. 4 (October, 1946), pp. 447–83.

PASSMORE, J. A. "Descartes, the British Empiricists and Formal Logic." *Philosophical Review* 62, no. 4 (October, 1953), pp. 545–53.

SMART, J. J. "Descartes and the Wax." *Philosophical Quarterly* 1 (October, 1950), pp. 50–57.

STOUT, A. K. "Descartes' Proof of the Existence of Matter." *Mind* 41 (April, 1932), pp. 191–207.

Index

225